A Better Vantage Point

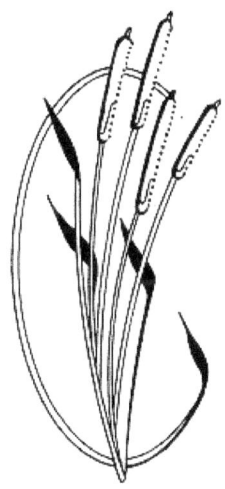

A Better Vantage Point

Pastor Eric Burr

Senior Publisher
Steven Lawrence Hill Sr

ASA Publishing Corporation

A Publisher Trademark Title page

ASA Publishing Corporation
An Accredited Publishing House with the BBB
www.asapublishingcorporation.com

The Landmark Building
23 E. Front St., Suite 103, Monroe, Michigan 48161

All Rights Reserved. No part of this publication may be reproduced, stored in a retrieval system or transmitted in any form or by any means electronic, mechanical, photocopying, recording or otherwise, without the prior written permission of the publisher. Author/writer rights to "Freedom of Speech" protected by and with the "1st Amendment" of the Constitution of the United States of America. This is a work of non-fiction. Any resemblance to actual events, locales, person living or deceased that is not related to the author's literacy is entirely coincidental.

With this title/copyrights page, the reader is notified that the publisher does not assume, and expressly disclaims any obligation to the authors own workings, within the author's rights as manuscript owner. Nor is the publisher obligated to obtain and/or include any other information other than that provided by the author (unless permitted) and within the ownership rights thereof. Any belief system, promotional motivations, including but not limited to the use of non-fictional/fictional characters and/or characteristics of this book, are within the boundaries of the author's own creativity in order to reflect the nature and concept of the book.

Any and all vending sales and distribution not permitted without full book cover and this copyrights page.

Copyrights
©2017 Pastor Eric Burr, All Rights Reserved
Book Title: A Better Vantage Point
Date Published: 09.24.2017 / Edition 1 *Trade Paperback*
Book ID: ASAPCID2380736
ISBN: 978-1-946746-19-1
Library of Congress Cataloging-in-Publication Data

This book was published in the United States of America
Great State of Michigan

A Publisher Trademark Copyrights page

ACKNOWLEDGEMENTS

I would like to thank so many people who have been such a tremendous support to me down through the years.

My Second New Hope Church family who day in and day out display the Love of God that we talk about and who rise to the occasion to help those in need, thank you.

To Pastor Jake Gaines who has been a friend and an encouragement to me to write this book, thank you.

My parents, James and Gladys Burr who lived daily, their life before me, to show me that I could achieve regardless of the oppositions and obstacles waiting to hinder me and still hold fast to God.

To my son Eric Emmanuel, granddaughter Kemory and grandson, Eric Ethan; thank you for your sacrifice. Many times you had to share me with the ministry. God has blessed me with you, and I love my blessing.

And to my wife, Odetta, who for the last thirty-three years have been walking along side of me every step of the way, even when the path was not always convenient. She has been my vision of the Proverbs 31, Virtuous Woman, thank you.

INTRODUCTION

How is your view of the world? What is your perspective on the condition of the world in your neighborhood, in your home and in your personal relationships? What is your vantage point for tomorrow, your outlook for the future? Is it bright and promising, or does the future for you look bleak, dismal and uncertain? Or, perhaps the question should not be what is your perspective, but do you even have a perspective, a vantage point on life to stand on, or have you yet to recognize that you are standing on the perspectives formed by others?

Let me say from the beginning that I do not have the artistic skills of Norman Rockwell, nor can I share the adventures that could compare with the adventures of Lewis and Clark, but if you would allow me, I would like to paint a portrait of a map that has taken me fifty years to paint.

I believe in my heart, despite all of our faults, failures, and short comings that I live in the greatest country in the world. We are great not only because of our military might and technology but also because of these truths that our forefathers so boldly proclaimed that all men are created equally and were endowed by their creator to life, liberty and the pursuit of happiness.

However, something went terribly wrong somewhere during the process between the proclamation and the practice. If I may paraphrase Maya Angelou and Martin Luther King Jr., these yet to be United States have written a check that has been returned stamped insufficient funds when it came to people of color. I grew up to witness with my own eyes a smoldering cross, a Klan rally in the small southern town in Georgia that I call my second home, and soldiers and tanks patrolled down city streets in Detroit during that hot summer of 1967 as a people cried, "no more!" I lived in a decade where we lost a president who challenged us to ask not what our country can do for us, but what we can do for our country, a time of war, and the movement of peace, hippies, love, drugs, Bobby, Malcolm, Martin, Medgar, and the innocence of Camelot, and yet, we are still here. Not only are we here, but we have also had the audacity to elect the first black president, forty years later.

I do not write this book as a condemnation of this great country. God has directed my steps down a certain path with a vantage point that through the years was registered and stored in my heart for such a time as this to be shared.

By definition to have a vantage is to have superiority over a competitor as in means of an attack or to have an advantage. A vantage ground is a position or condition that gives one an advantage against one's opposition. Militarily, a vantage point gives you the advantage against your enemy.

Many times we ignore seemingly insignificant events in our daily lives. The bible tells us in Romans 8:28 (KJV)

"And we know that all things work together for good to them that love God, to them who are the called according to his purpose."

As believers in our Lord and Savior Jesus Christ, we understand that events, good and bad, come into our lives. Being a Christian does not exempt problems large or small from settling on our front porch. And being a work in progress, I've learned that it's not the event that's the issue, because we all have our events in life. The question is how do you address and handle your event, for your good? Our individual vantage points can be as diverse and as distinct as our individual finger prints given to us at birth. It is developed and defined through our upbringing, education, relationships, world events, personal experiences, victories and our defeats in this life.

Often times in order to achieve a better vantage point requires us to join with like-minded and spirited individuals trying to reach that same goal.

Hopefully, as you read further, that vantage point may cause you to recognize overlooked or neglected events that have been intricately woven into the fabric of your life that may change your perspective of your vantage point for the better.

Table of Contents

BEST BLOCK USA 1

THE GREAT MOTIVATOR 7

MY VIEW THROUGH A TELESCOPE 14

WALK IN YOUR AUTHORITY 18

THE OBAMA FACTOR 23

O MAGNIFY YOUR VISION 30

NIGHT VISION 36

OPPORTUNITY TO EXCEL 41

HELP SOMEBODY 48

THE LITTLE CHURCH THAT COULD 51

A VIEW FROM THE ROAD 56

THE CUTLASS CLUB 62

RISE UP AND BUILD 67

SELLING UMBRELLAS 72

A VIEW FROM THE MOUNTAIN TOP 76

LEAVE IT ON THE FIELD 87

A VIEW FROM THE OWNER'S MANUAL 91

A Better Vantage Point

Pastor Eric Burr

BEST BLOCK USA

For the first five years of my life, I lived on a street in the inner city of Detroit named 16th street. I am the youngest of four siblings. I have an older sister and two older brothers. Not only were there the six of us living there, but I had two uncles who also lived with us. It was a small home with only one bathroom. It was often times a tight living arrangement, but we were family, and we made it work. We were not just a family in name only, we were a functional family who genuinely loved each other. I was too young to appreciate the family unit and often took it for granted until I got older, but my family understood that family was a blessing straight from God. Holidays were always a big event, especially Thanksgiving and Christmas. We were by no means wealthy, but Christmas was unbelievable. There were always so many gifts under the tree, and by me being the youngest, most were mine. Friends coming over would often ask if those were really gifts under the tree or just decorations, but they were all gifts. My father, for better or worse, worked two jobs to be sure that we had a great Christmas. There was this deep seeded sense of family that was instilled in my parents back in Georgia where they were raised, and that very spirit was passed on to us.

In the summer of 1964, I was a young energetic, five year old boy when my parents decided to move from our home on the west side of Detroit five miles away to the northwest side. Although we did not move far, I believe that our new home was right on the corner of best block USA. At the age of five, many things changed for me. My school had changed, the complexion of my neighborhood had changed, my prospects had changed, my present, and future associations had changed, and yes, my neighborhood had changed. All of these changes came together and met one another on a street named Prairie and helped form my vantage point for the rest of my life.

I'm sure that many of you would testify that your home set in the middle of Best Block, USA. It was on Prairie where I met my best friends in the world, friends that I have had for over 50 years, and although we've grown up and traveled down different roads, made new relationships and started our own families, to this day we still keep up with one another and are always just a phone call away. There were things that were placed in and around us that shaped the rest of our lives, things that we did not readily recognize or took for granted. Looking back over the years at all that has happened and where I stand now, that move from 5739 16th Street to Prairie had a large impact on me.

I had a friend that lived a couple of blocks over who referred to us as Prairie Dogs. I did not know it then, but there was a lot of truth in that name. Prairie Dogs live in large colonies or towns of several families where they look out for one another. Prairie Dogs will sound an alarm if danger was approaching to warn others. On Prairie, every home with children had a mother and a father. This was so important to me because although I also had a father, he worked two jobs, and his main one was working the afternoon shift. This meant that many times during the week he was at work when I was home, and when he was home, I was at school. However, on Prairie where I was raised, parents who took an active role in raising not only their own children but also each others. If you were over at dinner time, you were always invited to eat. If we were doing something that we had no business doing, they were always quick to stop us and correct us as they would their own. Depending on the severity of an offense, they would call home and tell momma what I done. If the ice cream truck was going by, they would buy us an ice cream. If my mother needed some eggs or anything, she could send me down the street to the neighbor, because if one had it, we all had it. Our parents would sit out on the porch during the summer and talk while keeping an eye on us well into the evening while we played. This attitude of village care and concern on Prairie reinforced the commitment of family and transcended beyond the walls of my home to others.

Jesus asked the question, "Who is my neighbor?" There laid a man who had been robbed and left for dead on the side of the road when a priest walked by without offering help. Then a scribe looked at him and passed by without helping. Then a Samaritan saw the man in trouble, stopped, and helped him. Jesus said that Samaritan who went over and beyond to help someone he did not know was the good neighbor. I took for granted that this act of care and concern for others was everywhere, but as I ventured out of my neighborhood, I found that attitude was far and few between. Not everyone cared or was even concerned enough to help someone else's child.

Although my new neighborhood was still predominately African American, there were other nationalities who did not look like me who lived there and raised their kids there. I attended Louis Pasteur Elementary School. Pasteur was a school that educated white and black kids. There were families who were well off financially and others who struggled. This diversity in race and economics taught me early about grace, mercy, and tolerance of others who were different. I believe that it was my 4th grade teacher that taught me a valuable lesson in bigotry. She asked all of the students who had brown eyes to stand up, and all of us who had brown eyes stood to our feet. Some of us were black and some of us were white. One by one she handed all of the brown eyed students a piece of candy. The students that did not receive candy proclaimed that was not fair. Some of them were white and some were black. Some had blue eyes, some green, and others, hazel. They were not good or bad, just different. They were not superior intellectually or financially, just different, but they were omitted simply because of the color of their eyes. That experience of discrimination at that young age had a profound effect on my view of others not like me, and that changed my vantage point. I chose to see past the obvious differences, to look for commonality, and to see the good layered underneath.

Moving to Best Block USA also changed my father's expectations for my future. My father worked in a steel mill full-time and cleaned a grocery store part time. Both of my brothers and my uncles worked in the factory. My father worked hard for everything and was thankful for the job that he had, and being the youngest in the family by eleven years, my father desired more for me. We lived four blocks outside of Sherwood Forest, an exclusive neighborhood where the houses were over the top, with private security guards patrolling the area, built in swimming pools, tennis courts and foreign cars. This is where many doctors, lawyers, and engineers lived. We saw opportunities to do more than just a factory job. We encountered people daily with an education earning more money, living in bigger homes, and driving nicer cars. Living on Best Block

USA changed my vantage point to see that there was more available to people regardless of their pigmentation, although there were still issues brewing when it came to race.

Many of us dare not to ask for more in life because we simply could not conceive of more. What we saw on television was Hollywood made for TV fantasy, or it is only for a select, privileged few. Getting more out of life is not just for the athletes. It's also for those who are ready to put in the work to be more than what is expected of them by the masses. My mother told me that I could achieve and become whatever I desired, and she provided me with the tools to make those dreams come true. My uncles were always that source of encouragement to think outside of the box. My uncle Curt said one way to help the poor was not to become poor. That sounded harsh but true. How can you help them when you're standing in need? And, if you make it, that's one less that needs help.

On Best Block USA, I had a great host of witnesses who were mentors, coaches, and cheerleaders for me outside of my family. They worked hard and paved the way for us to rise to the potential they seen in us. I had friends who applied positive peer pressure to press toward the mark of the high calling of Jesus Christ so I could run my race with patience and be able to obtain my goal. These were friends who were there on Best Block USA in 1964 and had my back growing up in Detroit and the same ones that I stood up at their weddings and who stood up at mine. These are the same few that I call my brothers and sit down with for breakfast to catch up with one another. This is my family from Best Block USA.

Looking at my life on Best Block USA caused me to look back and wonder, what if. What if my mother was not a good steward over the money that my father worked so hard to provide, we would not have been able to move that summer in 1964 from 16th street to Prairie. Three years after we moved during the summer of 1967 a police raid on an afterhours bar on 12th St and Clairmont resulted in the 67 riots. For five days in July, Detroit burned, 43 died and 1,189 people were injured. 2,509 businesses were looted or burned and 388 families were rendered homeless or displaced. The epicenter of the riots was 1 ½ miles from where we lived. I reflect and wonder what could have happened to my brothers, uncles or my parents had they got caught up in the chaos of the riots? My oldest brother had just returned from Viet Nam, serving this country. And as the riots raged where we grew up, he sat on the safety of our porch on Best Block and cried. After all that he had witnessed with the horrors of war on the other side of the world, only to come home and see his home burn. To this day, many parts of that area was never rebuilt. Many that could move out, did, and many of those left behind got caught up into the drugs, gang violence and the blight in that part of the city. The house on 16th St is nothing more than a memory now. If we had not moved in 1964, where would my mentors, coaches, support, and cloud of witnesses cheering me on have come from, and would I have the same vantage point that I possess now?

THE GREAT MOTIVATOR

Having a better vantage point often requires you identifying not just the best way for you to go, but understanding and seeing those paths that may give your adversary the advantage over you. What is it that has you motivated? What is that thing, that mechanism that moves you to action or freezes you in your footsteps? Your motivation will cause you to rise when the world says to sit, and cause you to push forward against all of the odds, oppositions, and obstructions that you may face. The great motivator will encourage you to take one more step when all logic and reason says that it's over. The great motivator will show you something that no one else can see.

However, your great motivator could cause you to throw in the towel and give up. It may cause you to stop at the first sign of opposition or obstacles in your path. Your great motivator may cause you to back track, retreat and run, or to trip and fall short of your goal.

When I was a young boy, I had a terrible fear of the dark. I had to sleep with all of my doors shut and the lights on. I never went downstairs alone at night for fear of the boogie man.

Fear is that monster that will paralyze you. That fear of the unknown will paralyze you. That thing that you do not know or do not understand will stop most of us from reaching or even attempting that goal, that dream that's been planted into our spirits. That dream that would elevate you and the people around you is being smothered and killed by a blanket of darkness called fear. That monster of fear wears so many hats that it's hard to keep track. The fear of failure that if you put in the time and energy, it might fail. The fear of rejection is that small voice that tells you that no matter how good the idea may be, there's no one who will see your vision and potential and it will be rejected. There's that fear that those who are close to you may reject your idea, and that leads to fear of loneliness. Fear will put you into a dark, lonely place. It's not that the darkness can harm you. It's that unknown factor of what's in the darkness. You can go into a dark room that's empty. You know it's empty, but you won't run through that room. No, you're gonna slow down, and your hands are gonna go up in front of you to protect you from the nothing in front of you.

Fear has a close relative, and they work very well together. Its name is "Doubt". Fear is that monster in your life that raises doubt, that deep-seeded, nagging thought that your dream is somehow inadequate and ill-conceived. Doubt raises that flag of uncertainty and second-guessing. Doubt is that monster that can and will come from the expected as well as the unexpected. You have those forces that you are aware are against you and that you see when they're coming at you. You see your adversary throwing the hand grenades of doubt at your attempts, your idea, and your plans. These adversaries can also be hatred, of you and everything that you are about. Many times your adversary can hate you and not really know themselves why. Hate is a motivator in itself.

History can be your messenger of doubt. Your personal history can cause doubt to rise up in you. The fact that you never tried something before can raise doubts. The fact that you may not have the experience of those around you may raise some doubts... At my job with the U.S, Army Corps of Engineers, I was part of a Leadership Development Program. There was a class in team building and problem solving. By using a set number of planks of wood, everyone had to cross from one side to the other without leaving anyone behind. There were engineers in the group trying to figure out the puzzle. Each attempt failed, one after another. While we were trying to figure out the problem that had us stumped, a secretary kept making a suggestion to solve the problem. Everyone was discounting and doubting her suggestion simply because she did not have the background of those in the group who were experts in their field. She could have given up and given in to the rejection, but she didn't. She kept on suggesting until someone finally listened, and it was she who saw what those who were supposedly superior could not.

Many times doubt arises from the very one who is close to you, not your enemy, but the one who loves you and would never do anything to purposely injure you. They have been conditioned by their own history of failed attempts. They will tell you that they tried that particular idea twenty years ago and it did not work then. They will tell you that the MAN will never let you do that. And my question is: who is this man that is bigger than my GOD? Who is this man that is greater than my GOD? Somebody show me this man who is greater than my GOD! For greater is He that is in me than he that is in the world. Jesus said that greater things we would do, but I believe that we allow doubt to stop us. Scientists say that is physically impossible for a bumble bee to fly. His body is too big for his short wing span for it to fly, but somebody forgot to tell the bumble bee. The enemy does not have to destroy you, but if he can somehow distract you or detain you long enough for you to miss your appointed and anointed time, he wins.

Numbers 14:30 King James Version (KJV)

> *Doubtless ye shall not come into the land, concerning which I sware to make you dwell therein, save Caleb the son of Jephunneh, and Joshua the son of Nun.*

Many of us will never enter our promise because we choose to believe our doubts and doubt our beliefs. Moses sent spies to check out the promised land and bring back a report. Their report was that the land was truly great and rich and flowing with milk and honey, but the people were as giants, there was no way they could conquer them, and that the Children of Israel should turn around and leave. All but Joshua and Caleb. Their report was similar, that it was rich and great, flowing with milk and honey, and the people are great, and we are as grasshoppers in comparison, Yes Moses, all of that is true, but we can take them. We can take the land. God had been with Israel through the ten plagues; He was with them as they crossed the Red Sea and He was with them as they witnessed all of Pharaoh's men drown in the very waters that they crossed on dry land, and yet they rather believed naysayers and believe that God brought them this far to leave them. It was this doubt that gave rise to their fears to trust in the same God that brought them this far, and all of those over the age of twenty-one years of age was not allowed to enter into the Promised Land.

Where fear and doubt delay and distract you from a better vantage point, greed can obscure your vision to see clearly the direction to proceed to get where God will have you.

Greed is a monster that takes on characteristics to drive you to do things that you never believed you could do. Greed removes the brakes of caution and lowers the boundaries of morality. Greed will lead you to lie, cheat, and steal. In a word, the scriptures call this monster: Evil.

1 Timothy 6:10 King James Version (KJV)

> [10] *For the love of money is the root of all evil: which while some coveted after, they have erred from the faith, and pierced themselves through with many sorrows.*

Let me say that money is not evil. Money is a tool to be used and used wisely. Just as you would be careful using a saw, for fear of severing a finger, caution is to be in place when using money, for you stand the risk of severing so much more than a finger. Greed has severed family ties and destroyed relationships between brothers and sisters and between husbands and wives. Greed gave rise to corruption and that corruption gave rise to the downfall of corporations, cities, states, and countries.

Just as doubt, fear and greed are motivators to distort and limit your vantage point, there are motivators at hand to give you clarity in the midst of distortion and remove the shackles that have restrained so many of us for so long. Faith brings into view those things that others may be unable to see or understand. It can sometimes become so clear to you that it becomes confusing as to why others cannot see what you see. But understand that this is your vantage point, given to you by God to get a glimpse of what's possible. And this vantage point is made clear because of faith.

Hebrews 11:1 (KJV)

> [11] *Now faith is the substance of things hoped for, the evidence of things not seen.*

Our faith is always under constant attack from our known enemies, enemies that you did not realize that you had or those close to you who cannot see your vision because their vantage point has been distorted or has not been developed to see what you see. I believe that this is why the writer of the book of Hebrews says, "Now Faith." This faith needs to be moveable, reinforceable and able to grow. The faith that I had yesterday was what I needed for that situation then, but today I need that NOW Faith to deal with the issues that are confronting me now. My NOW FAITH is the stuff that I hoped for, and although I cannot see it with my naked eye, I see it. With this faith I stand against my opposition. With this faith I can walk alone. With this faith, I continue to reach the unreachable, attain the unattainable and believe the unbelievable. I am not subscribing to a name it, claim it and blab it and grab it doctrine, but this faith will illuminate those paths necessary for me to reach my goal.

Faith is not the absence of recognizing danger. There is a great difference in recognizing a clear and present danger and possessing a spirit of fear. There were instances when the people wanted to take Jesus, but he removed Himself, for it was not His time.

And then there is the motivation called Love. Love is that force that the world does not understand. The world will write about and even sing about and avails itself of it without using the instruction manual that comes with it; the Holy Bible. The world have used, misused, and abused Love. It has been lied on, lied to, manipulated and molested. Love is often mistaken for being weak and vulnerable, but that could not be further from the truth.

Love is not stagnant, stale or antiquated, but Love is an action word. Love is kinetic, it moves, has energy, it lives and it grows.

1st Corinthians 13

> *Love suffereth long, and is kind; Love envieth not; Love vaunteth not itself, is not puffed up,*
>
> *Doth not behave itself unseemly, seeketh not her own, is not easily provoked, thinketh no evil;*
>
> *Rejoiceth not in iniquity, but rejoiceth in the truth; Beareth all things, believeth all things, hopeth all things, endureth all things. Love never faileth: but whether there be prophecies, they shall fail; whether there be tongues, they shall cease; whether there be knowledge, it shall vanish away.*

And Paul ends this chapter with;

Faith, Hope and Love, these three, but the greatest of these is Love.

Love is that motivator to drive you to continue further than you thought possible, when logic tells you to stop and the opposition says to give up. Love will tell you to hang in there when you're ready to throw in the towel. The vantage point of Love is that X-Factor that your opposition will many times overlook or underestimate when it comes to you hanging in there. Many consider love as predictable and a weakness to be manipulated and exploited by your enemies. And love can be characterized in many ways, predictable, maybe. Manipulated? Possibly, but not a weakness. Love moves and encourages those to keep pressing against those oppositions that faces us. Love is that ointment that gives comfort to the hurting and that reinforcement that strengthens hope against hope.

MY VIEW THROUGH A TELESCOPE

In 1990, NASA launched its Hubble Space telescope into low earth's orbit. This telescope allowed astronomers to view portions of the galaxy with depth and clarity, without the distortions caused by earth's atmosphere.

I remember receiving as a child a telescope for Christmas and it allowed me to look way out into the heavens and bring it closer to me to see with clarity those things that I could not see with my naked eye. One special Christmas God gave me a telescope to see something close up with unusual clarity that I had not seem before.

Every Christmas my family and I make our annual trek to Georgia to share the holidays with our families. My brother Jimmy and my in-laws live about five miles apart in a small town on the western edge of Georgia, called Temple, a small town with a population around 1500 with train tracks that run right through the middle of town. This is the town where my grandparents settled down and my mother was raised. The Christmas of 2003 was no different than the others. We had a great time enjoying one another's company, sharing, shopping, eating, and eating some more.

As we prepared to head home to Detroit, I packed my goodies as I usually do. I had my cookies, chips, soda and music strategically placed, ready to start my shift driving home. As we headed down the road on Highway 113 into the night, making our way north to Detroit, something different happened. Instead of turning on the music, to settle into my rhythm and cracking open some chips, I just drove and drove. I soon found myself off the two lane highway and on Interstate I-75, headed towards Chattanooga. The family had settled in and fallen asleep, and I still had not turned on the music or eaten any of the snacks. In the midst of the quiet and the solitude is when I heard from the Lord. I cannot say that it was an audible voice, but a voice that I understood just as loud and clear as if Odetta was sitting up and talking to me.

The voice of the Lord was directing me what to do. Although I was hearing Him, I was not comprehending. I was interrupting to explain that I was not a pastor and did not have the position, status, or authority to do what was being told to me. However, the voice kept telling me in no uncertain terms what I would do. There would be ministry to gather the men, ministry to those left behind, a ministry of Hope, and a ministry of Freedom. Nearly five hours after leaving my in-laws home in Temple, Georgia, and driving and talking with the Lord, I found myself through Tennessee and nearly to Lexington Kentucky. I was not a pastor to start any of the ministries that was planted into my spirit like a seed by the voice of God. For five months that seed laid dormant in me, waiting to grow and to one day provide fruit for harvest.

On the first Sunday in May 2004, we had another good Sunday service. As Pastor Lewis made final remarks before the benediction, he asked our visitors if they would excuse themselves because we had some church business to discuss. After the benediction and after the visitors had exited the sanctuary, my pastor gave his letter of resignation to the church. There was no scandal or problem. He said that this was as far as the Lord was taking him as pastor of Second New Hope. Pastor Lewis began the process of walking us through the journey of looking for a new pastor to lead the sheep at this church that I called home. Within about forty minutes I was unanimously selected to shepherd the Second New Hope Missionary Baptist Church into the future. The vision that was shown to me as I traveled Interstate 75 in late December 2003, heading for home, began taking focus.

Unable to eat, I took a walk. Although it was May and the weather was beautiful, I was walking like it was January after an ice storm where my steps were gentle and unsure with the fear of falling. As I walked with tears in my eyes, I asked God, now what? A gentle breeze blew against my face that told me to remember what I was shown, you and the more that I walked, the more I could remember. My steps got stronger, wider, and more confident. I wiped away the tears and was able to see more clearly the path before me and what I had to do. As I got home from the walk, I looked at Odetta and said that we had work to do. A few moments after I returned, Pastor Lewis called and said, "Son, you cannot let the congregation see you cry. You can cry in your office or at home, but the people are shaken right now and they need your strength."

As I look back on that trip home, I realize that God had allowed me to take a special glimpse through the lens of a telescope to see just a portion of what was to come. That glimpse through that telescope let me get a closer view in vivid color and detail, of what was possible. My view through the telescope let me see the possible, past the distortions and distractions and the obstacles that comes with the atmosphere of life. And just as NASA had issues and problems with Hubble and corrections had to be made to bring the universe into the clarity that we observe today, I had to make adjustments and corrections to deal with unanticipated distortions and distractions surrounding me, that would cause me not to see as clearly as I should. My issues were not with the telescope, but with the distractions around me. Members in trusted positions, unexpectedly leaving, because of their personal ties to Pastor Lewis. I took and viewed their leaving as a personal indictment against me, but God had to show me that it was not about me. Those that left the church, who could not come to terms with another man sitting in their Spiritual Father's chair. The one who had led, counseled, encouraged, and provided them with their spiritual and physical nourishment was gone. They supported me as long as I was the assistant to Pastor Lewis, but once I became Pastor, things changed.

They maintained the respect for the office, but I was like a new step father who was sitting in the seat of the man who introduced them to Christ, who threw them that spiritual life preserver, that kept them afloat during the storms of their lives and they could not come to terms with me or God for the change in leadership or direction.

Even as believers in Jesus Christ, change can be difficult to handle in our own understanding. We often look for signs and wonders in the most grandiose manner, like the parting of the Red Sea, as Moses, and the children of Israel crossed on dry ground, or the falling of the walls of Jericho as the children marched around in obedience to God. But many times it's not something so grand but in a quiet whisper during that private time with the Lord that He can bring that thing that seems to be so far away, up close with all clarity to reach out and grab a better vantage point.

When things in life appear to get fuzzy and out of focus, I try to go back to that telescope to view what God wants for me to see and not those around me who wants me to see the possibilities through the lens that they have prepared. Their telescope maybe good and even possibly focused on those things of heaven, but that does not necessarily mean that their telescope is focused from the vantage point of what God would have for me to see or even reach for. Pastor Lewis said in his resignation that the Lord has taken him as far as he was to go as the pastor of Second New Hope. God did not call me to the pastorate to circle around like an airplane in a holding pattern, looking for a place to land, but has given me a view through the telescope positioned with a vantage to navigate His church to explore and discover and to share with others, what is still possible and how great God is.

WALK IN YOUR AUTHORITY

    I have always had an affection for those in authority. I have always had a great respect for seniors. I loved to sit down and listen to them because they had such a way of sharing so much. They may not have had much in the way of a formal education, but what they had to share has taken me where my education could not. My father only had a 6th grade education, but he was the smartest man in the world to me. He worked hard everyday, walked with God, and used common sense. Daddy would say that common sense is not so common, and the older I get, the more that I understand what he was talking about. There are some things that I see and it makes me scratch my head with amazement and wonder what made that person do what they did. When I first began my journey as a minister of the gospel of Jesus Christ, my Pastor, Rev. Gabriel Lewis told me that besides him, as much as possible I should try to hear two of his dear friends in the ministry: Rev. Tellis Chapman and Rev. E. L. Branch. And I made it my business to hear them as much as possible when they were in revival, locally.

    Sometimes people in passing can drop nuggets of wisdom right in your lap that can profoundly impact your life. However, the problem is that all too often we are so busy that we fail to recognize the value that those few words possess, and we will run off to the next meeting, the next recital, the next ball game, or the next movie and allow that precious piece of knowledge to hit the ground, never to be seen again. In order to recognize those valuable pieces of advice that come along in our lives, we need to slow down.

    My Pastor, Rev. Gabriel Lewis Sr, told me when I first started this walk of ministry, to observe all things. He said "Son, God is going to take things that you have seen everyday of your life and out of the ordinary reveal His Word in the form of a message to share with God's children, a word so bright to illuminate the lives of those who hear it, in such a way that will draw them closer to God and will guide them to where God would have them to be." Pastor Lewis said that it may be that same ole stop sign at the end of your street, a dripping faucet in your bathroom, or simply an evening rain beating on your window sill that God will provoke a word in you to share with the world. I can say that God has truly shown me through these years so much to help those who are willing to listen, beginning with me. And in helping them, it has allowed me to grow in areas that I never conceived of. I have made it my business to slow down and listen to what is going on around me.

God, in His infinite wisdom and power created the heaven and the earth. His first recorded words were, "Let there be light," and in the time span of thought, it was. And God created the sun and the moon, the majestic mountains, and the meandering streams. He spoke to the earth and the earth brought forth vegetation. He spoke again and the earth brought forth every bug and every beast big and small. God spoke to the waters and the waters brought forth every fish and every fowl. But when it came to create man, God spoke to Himself and said let us make man in our image and our likeness. And God formed man from the dust of the ground and blew into his nostrils the breathe of life, and man became a living soul. And God made man a little lower than the angels and gave him dominion over the world.

In November of 2004, I was five months into my pastorate and hosting my first revival. Our evangelist was Rev E. L. Branch, the proud Pastor of the Third New Hope Baptist Church. Being the spiritual brother of my spiritual father in the ministry, Rev Gabriel Lewis, I call Pastor Branch my spiritual uncle. And this relationship has afforded me certain access and privileges others do not have: his time, his insight, and his wisdom. On the first day of the revival,

Pastor Branch shared something with me that helped navigate my ministry with a better vantage point that all of his years of ministry has placed within him. He looked at me and told me some words that were so simple yet so profound to me. As we set in my office, he looked at me and said to "Walk in the Authority that God had given you. Not Branch, not Lewis, but Burr. The day that I stepped on that floor as pastor, I had more experience than anyone in that sanctuary". God had given me a path to walk down and this path was cleared for me. It was up to me to walk it. Branch said that "the day you walked on that sanctuary floor as pastor, you had more seniority than everyone in there."   Those few words to me were so timely in my life that I often find it difficult to even articulate the words to express it.

As Paul wrote to the church at Ephesus, Pastor Branch was telling me that God had chosen me before the foundation of the world and had predestined me through adoption that we should live holy before God. Walking in your authority will give your vantage point better clarity to navigate through the challenging decisions that we face in a fog of chaos and confusion.

While on vacation we took an Alaskan cruise. When we arrived in Seattle it was sunny and 80 degrees. But when we boarded the ship to depart for Alaska the forecast had changed to cloudy skies, rain, and 60 degrees. Six hours into the cruise those 80 degree temperatures were a memory that had been replaced by choppy waters, rain, and fog that kept our visibility confined to the ship we were sailing. That change in weather caused me to reflect on some things. I can imagine great joy and celebration by the disciple when Jesus healed the man possessed by a spirit as once again Jesus delivered another soul bound by circumstances out of his control. I imagine high fives going all around as they boarded the ship. I imagine sunshine days, calm waters, and a gentle breeze at their back as the ship left the dock. It was not long before the sunshine was replaced by darkness, that gentle breeze at their back was now the strong wind of opposition, and the high fives were replaced by fear and anxiety.

In life we are going to face storms. I don't care how holy you think you may be, storms are gonna come. Not maybe, or possibly, storms are definitely coming your way. Being in church everytime the doors swing open does not exempt you from the trials of the storm. Things may be going your way right now, so praise God for the good days. However just as the weather can change abruptly, life's circumstances can also. Sometimes when those changes come, our vision can be obscured. Things that have been consistent have now been shifted and not where it should be.

I love this technology we have today. A GPS is an acronym for Global Positioning System. A string of satellites in space are arranged to triangulate and locate your position to plot a course to drive. Although you cannot see the GPS, the GPS is always looking at you. It will track you at night, or sunshine or rain, clear skies or cloudy. All you have to do is type where it is that you want to go and the GPS system will navigate your every turn from point A to point B to get you to your destination. If you miss a turn, the GPS will tell you to turn around to get back on track. If you continue in the wrong direction, the GPS will recalculate the directions according to your new location and give you new directions to reach your destination.

Proverbs 3:5-6

> *[5] Trust in the Lord with all thine heart; and lean not unto thine own understanding.*
>
> *[6] In all thy ways acknowledge him, and he shall direct thy paths.*

In life, if you get off course and head into the wrong direction, either by mistake or intentionally, the Lord sees where you are and can recalculate where you need to be and provide you with a new set of directions. Your situation may be cloudy, foggy, or a torrential down pour. He will be there. He promised to never leave us nor forsake us, but can you trust Him and lean on Him as He directs your path?

Life, circumstances and situations can and will change quickly, but understand that the devil has no authority over you. He has power and he slick, cunning, a cheat, and seeking whom he may devour, but he has no authority over you!

THE OBAMA FACTOR

In 2008 I kept hearing about a young, articulate, polished, young man who happened to be African American, and who had the audacity to run for the highest office in the world. Barack Hussein Obama dared to do what most have only dreamed of achieving when we were children. People of all nationalities were blown away by his good looks and charisma as he rose in popularity to rock star status. Being a Baptist preacher, I enjoyed his oratory presentation and command of the audience, but I was looking deeper for the meaning in his message. I had serious doubts about choosing this man to be my commander in chief. I had reservations about his ability to lead. I heard arguments on both sides that said that I would vote for Obama solely because he and I shared the same ethnicity. We were both African American. Some did not vote for him because they were concerned for his safety from those who were not ready to accept a person of color to lead the greatest nation in the world.

When I made my decision to vote for that the young man from Chicago, by way of Hawaii, I did not vote for him because he was a black man, and I didn't discount him out of concern for his safety, although both reasons gave me reason to pause and ponder. I voted for him because I believed that this man of Black and White ancestry had the ability to draw opposite opinions together, to reach across party lines, and make a difference. I believed that this man was articulate enough, polished enough, informed, and compassionate enough to get it done. He continually displayed the demeanor of Jackie Robinson when publicly confronted by opposition. Many times during the debates when his opponent replaced fact with fiction, he tilted his head, smiled, stayed focused, and continued with his debate. He refused to climb into the mud and fight at the level of his opponent. He took the high road, even when he had the opportunity to sling mud. This encouraged me and eventually sold me on Barack Obama.

On Tuesday, November 4, 2008, I flew out of Chicago before the election polls closed and headed home from a business trip. That evening as I walked into my living room where my family was watching the election results, my son hollered out, "DAD he's winning, he's taking it to him!" Although his assertion was premature, something awesome was happening right before my eyes. As I sat there and watched the returns come in, it happened. They announced that Mr. Barack Obama had been elected the first African American to the presidency of the United States of America. As the announcement resonated in my living room and in my heart, my mind went back to my grandparents in the mid 60s in rural Temple Georgia and the struggles that this country endured because of prejudice. I thought about the smoldering cross that I witnessed my on that red dirt road. I thought about the Klan marching in that small town that I loved in 1992. I thought about all of the fallen leaders who had paved the way, such as Martin Luther King, Jr, Robert Kennedy and President JFK. I thought about the marches, the lynchings, the hopes, dreams, and aspirations of a people. I thought about those who have gone on to glory without seeing this day. I knew in my heart that this moment would one day happen, but I never thought it would happen in my lifetime. And as I stood there with tears running down my face, it did. He had made the impossible, possible. Through all of the fears, speculations, and misconceptions, the polls said that it was time for a change.

Across this country, around the world, from Chicago to Detroit, to Africa and Asia and all points in between, people were dancing in the streets with a renewed sense of hope. On Wednesday morning I was off to Nassau the Bahamas to attend the Kingdom Builders Pastors and Peoples International (KBPPI) Conference. As we deplaned the aircraft, with my wife still wearing her Obama pin, the Bahamian people started cheering. I asked a young Bahamian lady what was going on? She told me, "Sir, we love Obama here in the Bahamas!" Everywhere we traveled in the Bahamas, the citizens cheered about what had happened in America.

Throughout his campaign Mr. Obama preached change. The direction that the nation was headed needed a course correction. We have to change our course, our actions and our way of doing business. If this nation was going to return to its glory, we must, not an option, but we must make a change. When I returned from the KBPPI conference and spoke to the congregation for the first time since that historic election night, I told the church that once the dust settled, once all of the dancing has ceased and all of the party decorations have been put away, that our newly elected president was expecting everyone to make a change. For some reason many people of color, those in the minority, those with less financial resources, and the have nots were expecting the haves to make all of the changes. However, if there was going to be any real and lasting change, then WE as a People have to be ready to stop pointing the finger of blame at someone else and pause long enough to take a long, hard look in the mirror and be prepared to make a change ourselves.

2 Corinthians 13:5 (KJV)

⁵ Examine yourselves, whether ye be in the faith; prove your own selves. Know ye not your own selves, how that Jesus Christ is in you, except ye be reprobates?

To have a better vantage point, we must be willing to honestly examine ourselves. We are living in a microwave age where life is moving around us faster and faster everyday and becoming more difficult to juggle and navigate our way through. It is imperative that we make time to take a closer look at ourselves to see if we are part of the solution or a part of the problem. Ask yourself, am I a help or a hindrance to my surroundings? Are you here to set up and establish the road blocks of opposition, or are you here to help pave the road of opportunities to excel? Change can be awkward, clumsy, uncomfortable, difficult, and maybe even impossible to achieve if you cannot see your part in the equation. I counsel with couples and have learned that there are usually three sides to the problems in their relationship, His side, Her side, and the side of the Truth. It's usually never a one-sided problem, but issues on both sides. It's easier to highlight the others' faults, failures, and shortcomings in the relationship than to turn the spotlight of blame on yourself and admit that there's plenty of blame to go around. Change can only come when we first acknowledge that change is needed and that it needs to start with us. President Obama had the unmitigated gall, and audacity to dare to dream to become more than what the status quo told him was possible. He has risen up to lead the most powerful country in the world during some of the most difficult times in recent history.

What the president did was to remove that crutch that had been propping up to many of us for too long. We have held on to that crutch for so long that it appeared to have become a part of us. We've become accustomed to the cliché that, "The Man Won't Let you do That," or "I Tried That Before and it Won't Work," or "You'll Never Make It," and too many of us have not only heard it, but we have also bought into an existence of apathy and quit before we even started. As I look at back in our history, there were so many who began their journeys with meager means, but with aspirations and grit and a dogged determination, they rose to the highest heights because they had a better vantage point to see, what others would or could not see and they managed to maintain their focus and claim the prize.

I am fully aware that there are those who want people of color to remain in a certain social class and their aim is to provide every obstacle possible to keep us there. Yes, there will be challenges, obstacles, doubters, and haters who will try to cloud your vision and make your way dark, but at some point in time we have to rid ourselves of the crutch of excuses that only partially propped us up, but still left us stagnant and hindered from reaching where God would have us to be. I want somebody to show me this man that we talk about, that's bigger than my GOD! Show me this obstacle that my GOD cannot get me over! Show me this problem that is so great that my GOD cannot overcome.

"For I can do all things through Christ which strengthens me"!

One day in 1955 a tired young lady named Rosa Parks decided to sit, but when she sat down, she was actually taking a stand. Because Rosa stood, a King was able to march and dream dreams of a better day, and because Martin Luther King marched, Barack Obama was able to Run!

We often talk about Dr. King's last speech before he was taken from us. He said that I've been to the Mountain Top and I've Seen the Promised Land, but let me tell you that if you want to see the Promised Land for yourself, then you are going to have to do some climbing on your own. That means going up the rough side of the mountain. That terrain is often steep and uneven, uncertain and tiring, but you have to keep on pushing. How many times was President Obama told that he could not make it? How many times was he told to give up? How many times was he told that he was dreaming a fool's dream only to keep pressing and pushing against the naysayers and negativity to achieve what most thought was impossible?

And to reach that unreachable and utterly unattainable plateau requires that you examine yourself and hold fast to your faith in God that "All things are possible through Christ if you only believe." This is not a free ride, but it's going to cost you and cost you dearly. It's going to cost you your time, your talent, and your treasures. It's going to cost your blood, sweat and many tears. It's may cost you many of your loved ones along the way who could not see what you see to get where you're going.

Do you have that faith to believe the unbelievable, to reach the unreachable, and to attain the unattainable? Can you dare to trust in God more than man? Do you have the faith to believe what the Lord has shown you? Do you have the faith to see you buying your own home, the faith to go back to school, the faith to start your own business, or the faith to pursue those dreams that you thought were just that, dreams?

Please understand that no one person can reach that plateau all by themselves. It also involves those around you who believe enough in you to help. God will provide you with the resources and the support that you need to keep on pressing for the prize. However, all too often we give in to those who tell us that the road is too rough to navigate. This is why it is so important that we surround ourselves with those who are willing to invest in us: Positive, Progressive and Persistent people to encourage us, and just some yes men to agree with us, but those who are willing to also give constructive criticism. The president often speaks about the encouragement that he received from his mother. She did not see him reach the oval office, but always encouraged him to keep on striving against the odds. Moreover, the world has seen the strength and love of his wife, Michelle, to stand there with him to reach and grab hold of the impossible. Mr. Obama has kicked away those excuses for not pressing, not pushing, or striving to be more than what the world expects. He pressed past the naysayers and negativity to lead a people who many times did not want to be led. If you have the faith of a mustard seed, you will be able to move mountains and once you reconcile that notion in your head and your heart to engage your actions, your outlook for tomorrow will improve because you've changed your vantage point.

O MAGNIFY YOUR VISION

Growing up, I did what most boys did. I played baseball, basketball and football, thinking I would be the next superstar to hit the winning home run in the ninth inning to win the world series or catch a touchdown in the corner of the end zone to win the super bowl and be inducted into the hall of fame. From playing cowboys and Indians to wrestling, I did it. From racing to exploring the neighborhood, to riding my bike all the way downtown, I did it. I got in serious trouble for that one. I was going to be the next lead singer of the Temptations, an architect, a scientist, or an inventor; I believed that I could do it. Ironically, preaching never crossed my mind. Hmm.

One day my parents brought me a science kit, and in this kit was a magnifying glass. I found myself outside investigating everything from leaves to bugs. I discovered that if I adjusted the magnifying glass up or down that I could increase the intensity of the power of the sun on that object. And I discovered that if I focused the sunlight on dried leaves, I could actually start a fire.

Psalm 34 King James Version (KJV)

> *I will bless the Lord at all times: his praise shall continually be in my mouth.*
>
> *My soul shall make her boast in the Lord: the humble shall hear thereof, and be glad.*
>
> *O magnify the Lord with me, and let us exalt his name*

together.

This revelation taught me a valuable lesson to adjust my perspective and intensify my vantage point. Many times our view of life, relationships with one another and God is limited by our perspective of the one being observed. The scriptures tell us to Magnify the Lord with me. The scripture is precise and correct. Brothers and sisters, God is God and we don't have the power or the resources to make God bigger or smaller than what He already is. It was He who made us and not ourselves. But it is in our power to change our perspective of Him. By adjusting and focusing our view more onto God, it will increase our understanding and our dependence on Him, who has all power and the resources to fix and resolve our issues. Adjusting my perspective of God helps me to obtain a better vantage point of my relationships, personal and professionally. As well as the world as a whole. I understand that the world was formed by God and as chaotic as things may appear, He is still in control. Knowing that God is in control tempers my reaction to events out of my control. I did not have that sense of panic that seems to grab others. I don't minimize it or discount it, but recognize and realize that God has it under control. Although things appear to be catastrophic in nature, I know that God has me. On September 10, 2001, no one would have ever believed or imagined what was going to happen the very next day, but the unimaginable happened. Eyes were fixed on their television as fear and uncertainty set our perspective as terrorists hijacked four jet planes and flew two into the World Trade Center, one into the Pentagon and the forth into a Pennsylvania field after the brave passengers fought and died saving the victims at the fourth target. That following Sunday, churches all across the country were filled because of the acts of terrorist. My outrage, anger, and disbelief that something like this could happen to America, rose up in me like it did everyone, but God, who is rich in mercy, gave me a sense of calm in the midst of chaos and confusion that I could not do on my own. There's nothing like a traumatic event to cause people to reassess their views and vantages personally, as a nation, the world as a whole and even to reassess our views of God and our relationship with Him. Churches of all denominations across the country were filled with people for various of reasons. There were those who were filled with fear following the events of 911, those consumed with anger and the desire to strike back at the evil that has done this. There were those who needed that comfort from God to deal with this, and there were those who wanted to know where was God and how could God allow something like this to happen to us? We are the self proclaimed ambassadors of democracy, liberty and Christianity. We are that beacon of hope that shines its light of opportunity and prosperity to guide the masses to that better life.

Ironically, America is facing an identity crisis brought on by our own self righteous, superior attitude and our view of other countries and of God. As a young nation, we looked to God for direction and guidance in our growth and development. We grew and matured quickly in stature, might, wisdom and generosity in helping others to live the dream, realizing that it was not done by us alone, but by the hand of God keeping us. But, the more of a world leader that America became in the eyes of the world, the more we appeared to lessen our dependence, desire and our need for God. We were a country that proudly proclaimed that we were "Endowed by Our Creator," that we were "One Nation Under God" and a country who prominently displayed on our currency that "In God We Trust." We have managed to take prayer out of our schools, along with growing movements to remove our belief in God from the halls of those elected to govern this county and label those holding fast to their faith as fanatics. We are systematically telling God that He is no longer needed or necessary and have for all intent and purposes have asked Him to leave the very shores that He allowed us to occupy.

And now that He has removed the hedge from around us that has protected and sustained us for two hundred forty years and the unthinkable happened, we have the audacity to ask, where is God? God is where He has always been, seeking to love and care for His children. He simply gave America a taste of what we asked for and we are learning the hard way that life without God leaves a bitter taste in our mouths. It may not be totally accurate or even fair, but personally, going to school during the time when prayer was removed from our schools as it was, I've witnessed the decline of the education and the increase of violence and drug activity with our children.

The campaign platform that our 45th president, Donald Trump, ran on was to "Make America Great Again." He fed into the fears and doubts of a people that the other party neglected or discounted. Well, we are still a great nation! Do we have problems? Absolutely. Can we become greater? Without a shadow of a doubt. We still have more people trying to get into this great country that we love than those trying to leave.

2 Chronicles 7:14 King James Version (KJV)

> *[14] If my people, which are called by my name, shall humble themselves, and pray, and seek my face, and turn from their wicked ways; then will I hear from heaven, and will forgive*

their sin, and will heal their land.

If this country is going to rise to the level of greatness and stature that we have held and so carelessly dropped, we as a people have to refocus our perspective of God and His relevance to not just our world standing, but our very existence. I believe that the demise of this country will not come from an enemy outside of our borders, but from the very enemy within. We will be our own undoing. America's diet of riotous living, corruption, greed, and immorality is contrary to the will of God and we have slowly but surely eaten away the very fabric that has held us together since our birth as a nation. We have to, not an option, humble ourselves before God. Pride goes before the fall and great will the fall be if we do not align ourselves and actively seek our Creator.

Please understand that to whom much is given, much is also required. With the greatness that We the People have enjoyed down through the years, comes a great responsibility to help those who are in need. Should we secure our borders and vette those trying to enter? Absolutely, but we cannot let fear dictate how we treat those trying to find refuge. This country is filled with refugees who came from different regions and with different backgrounds who have stood together to build the United States of America. Jesus was a refugee who fled to Egypt to escape a crazed king. My faith in God is not diminished or diluted because of others who believe differently than I do. I am strengthened and resolute in my walk with the assurance of Jesus Christ and do not apologize for my affirmation. O Magnify the Lord with me and let us exalt His Name together!

It is with this assurance that gives believers a better vantage point to recognize potential problems and obstacles in their paths, to circumvent around them or endure the journey through them. It is with this vantage point that allows us to remain optimistic with the possibilities in front us, regardless of how daunting the task may appear to be. The hymn writer wrote:

"Blessed assurance, Jesus is mine; Oh, what a foretaste of glory divine. Heir of salvation, purchased of God. Born in His Spirit and washed in His blood. This is my story, this is my song, Praising my Savior all the day long."

NIGHT VISION

On June 18, 2013, I went to work as I did the day before and the week before that. I went through the day not feeling well, but working all the same. As it was time to leave for the day, I shut down my computer and stood up to go home, but things around me seemed off. I was not sure what it was, but things were off. I made it home alright and laid down to rest, hoping that I would feel better. I woke up around 11 PM to use the restroom, but when I stood up, things were not better, but worse. Everything seemed to be a varying shade of orange in color. I knew at that point that I had to go to the doctor in the morning. When I woke up around 8 in the morning, all I could see were shadows. No details, no colors, just shadows. It was like waking up in the middle of the night and seeing the outline of the furniture in the room, but no detail.

As Odetta and I were walking to the car to go to the doctor, I asked her if the sun was shining, and she replied yes. I could feel the heat of the sun on my face, but I could not see the sun. My doctor's office was closed on Wednesday, so I was directed to go straight to Emergency. The hospital staff took me right in and began asking me a lot of questions about my health and my family's health. They ran a battery of tests to determine what was going on. They ran tests for glaucoma, diabetes, a stroke, and multiple sclerosis. They ran an MRI, a Cat Scan, and a Spinal Tap looking for answers. One by one the tests came back negative. I was later asked by several people if I was afraid or told that experience must have been scary and strangely enough, my answer was no. I had this strange sense of calm about everything that was going on. As they continued to run test after test, I asked if they could see better if they turned on the lights. Odetta answered that every light was on in the room. It was at that time that I realized I was blind. The shadows had left and all I could see was the black of darkness. It was at that moment in the room when there was the deafening sound of absolute quiet. I was blind.

I had Odetta call my oldest brother, Jimmy, in Temple Georgia, to tell him what was going on. It was at that time that I became overwhelmed with emotions, broke down, and cried. I struggled to tell him what I did not understand myself as to what was happening to me.

It was if the Lord dropped a thought into my spirit, the story of Jonah, and I told him that I was going to stay in the belly of this fish for three days and see where the Lord spits me up. In the belly of a fish it is dark and desolate. You're isolated, alone, and uncomfortable. I was in a room full of people who loved me and were there to help me, and I had the ability to call anyone that I needed or wanted to call. As much as my family loved me and was there for me as I went on this journey, I was in a dark place. I did not know why or even where I would end up at the end, but I knew that I was not alone.

Hebrews 13:5-6

> [5] *Let your conversation be without covetousness; and be content with such things as ye have: for he hath said, I will never leave thee, nor forsake thee.*

⁶ So that we may boldly say, The Lord is my helper, and I will not fear what man shall do unto me.

God says that He would never leave me nor ever forsake me. I've learned that there are many of us who are living in a dark, isolated place, a place of confusion, chaos and turmoil. Many times we're in this dark place and do not realize it. We'll wander around aimlessly for years trying to find some clarity and direction in life. However, there comes a time when you have to sit still and wait on the lord and know that His Word is true. He will never leave you or turn His back on you in your time of need. I asked a friend and the church trustee if she would bring me a notebook to write some things down. Her response to me was Pastor, you can't see and my response back was that I can still write and when my sight comes back, I'll have plenty to talk about. I asked another friend, Reverend Michael Harris, to bring a friend to see me. Johnny has this heart for all of God's children. He genuinely has affection and love for family and friends, and although I was blind, I needed for Johnny to see that I was okay.

On the third night of my journey in the belly of my fish, I woke up around 4 o'clock in the morning, and just as my vision had left me, it had come back. I could see the television on the wall and the wall chart that had my name on it. I could see the curtains that divided me from the other patient. I could see! All I could think or say was THANK YOU JESUS! That's when the tears really ran down my face. No tears of pain or even fear, but tears of joy, praise, and thanks. Now those lyrics that I heard growing up as a child rang loud and with new understanding and clarity in my spirit. Amazing Grace, how sweet the sound, that saved a wretch like me. I once was lost, but now I'm found. Was blind, but now I see!

When Odetta got to my room, the first thing that she did was to take down the sign over my bed that the staff had placed there saying, the patient is blind." The doctors had no reason or explanation as to how my vision left or how it miraculously returned.

On the fourth night of my stay at the hospital, I received a special visitor. It was around four o'clock in the morning when I was awakened by a voice calling me. She was a dark complexed woman dressed in nurses attire. She had a Caribbean accent. She stood at the curtain dividing my bed from the gentleman in the other bed in the room. She spoke not in a whisper or in secrecy but in a normal tone, having a normal conversation. When she called me, she did not say Mr. Burr or Eric, but she addressed me as man of God. I had not told anyone that I was a preacher, but she addressed me as a Man of God. This woman told me that everything was going to be all right. Several times she assured me that I was okay, but I needed to get my rest. She told me that there was great work for me, but I needed my rest. There was no tension or anxiety in either one of us, but a sense of peace and calm. I told her okay and went right back to sleep. I did not think about that conversation any more till I headed home from the hospital. As Odetta was driving home from the hospital, the conversation came back to me. I was puzzled that throughout that conversation at four o'clock in the morning the gentleman in the next bed did not wake up. During my entire stay at the hospital, I had not seen her before the conversation or after. She simply came to me to assure me that everything was in order. Then she was gone. As I was heading home from the hospital, the question arose in my spirit, who was I talking to? I believe that I was talking to an angel.

Hebrews 13:1-2
> *¹³ Let brotherly love continue.*
>
> *² Be not forgetful to entertain strangers: for thereby some have entertained angels unawares.*

The scriptures tell that we ought to be mindful when we talk to strangers because you just don't know whom you're talking to and they just may be an angel sent by God.

As a young child, I was taught a song at my church that said, "All Day, All Night, Angels watching over me, My Lord." I believe that God dispatched a messenger to His child to give me some clarity when my physical vision was in question. I can't explain what happened to me that week in June. The doctors could not tell me what happened to me, but I believe there is a doctor who knows what happened and sent His nurse to watch over me. Many times, it's when it's the darkest in your life that you can see the farthest. It's in those darkest moments that we can see the stars that are always there but hidden by the light of the day. Sometimes we need the darkness of adversity to appreciate a clearer vantage point of where we are and where it is that we should be headed. I've learned through my journey to appreciate all that sight has to offer. There's so much that we take for granted when it comes to those things that we do everyday. I've learned to be more compassionate to those who do not see, not only physically, but also spiritually, those who cannot see the pitfalls on their path, dangerous turns, and bumps in the road because they don't have the vantage point to see the trouble that's waiting for them.

OPPORTUNITY TO EXCEL

Learning is an intricate part of living. A thread woven through the fabric of our lives that connects pieces together to make the whole. King Solomon tells us, "that with all of your getting, get an understanding." I have been taught that there is power in knowledge. Some run to learning for various and personal reasons, some for financial gain, and others for promotion on their jobs. For others it's a sense of accomplishment to learn. Where there are those who ran to gain knowledge, there were others who were pushed to learn. There was no personal motivation like promotion or some personal accomplishment to learn, but out of necessity that we were forced to get an education. These motivations alone were vantage points that was shaped within us early in life. Because of circumstances growing up in the rural south, my parents did not have much in the way of an education, but they understood the importance of learning. However, our education does not happen in the safety and security of a classroom room setting, but in the unsecured and often chaotic classroom of life.

Many times in life our better vantage point may not look better in the beginning. As a matter of fact, it often appears as if you may have made a wrong turn. You done all that you were supposed to do, and yet you find yourself in an awkward and uncomfortable position. Job was a man who was richer than most could imagine. He had it all: Fortune, Respect, Status, Fame, and Family, but most of all, he had God. Job was upright and righteous in the eyes of God.

Job avoided evil, prayed daily, and walked in the Lord's way. He prayed on behalf of his children, just in case they messed up and fell into sin.

Job was living the life that others dreamed of when without warning everything that he had obtained and worked for was gone. All of his livestock was stolen, all of his servants taken and his ten children were killed. His body was stricken with boils, and his wife, in her anguish, told Job to curse his God and die. With all of his loss, Job replied that "naked I came into this world and naked I shall return. The Lord giveth and the Lord taketh away, blessed be the name of the Lord." Wow, what a testimony! To lose everything and to still have the vantage point to see that all that he had, came from God and was able to give God the praise in the midst of his loss and suffering. Job is teaching us that being a child of God does not exempt trials into the life of a believer, but those trials can reshape your perspective to give you a better vantage point to deal with adversity when it comes your way. In the midst of adversity and the appearance of defeat and despair when it may be easier to give up and give in to what has happened to you, with a better vantage point is an opportunity to excel.

January 10, 1974, should have been just another Thursday morning, to get up and head to school as I had done the day before. However, I was awakened to loud conversation between my mother and my brother, Freddie. Momma was on the phone trying to calm Freddie down as he was hysterically telling her that our eldest brother, Jimmy, had gotten his leg cut off in a factory accident. When Momma tried to get off of the phone with Freddie, she believed that it wasn't that bad and was probably nothing more than a broken leg. She was assuring me that he was alright and Freddie's imagination had gotten the best of him. However, his imagination was not exaggerated as Jimmy's leg had been severed in an accident. The right leg had been severed and his left leg had been badly damaged as well. It would have been easier to simply remove the leg and begin rehabilitation, but the ambulance took him to Bi-County hospital where the doctor on staff believed that the leg could be saved, and Dr. Rook proceeded to reattach that leg that had so violently taken from him. While all of this was happening, his wife, Emma, was seven months pregnant with their third child. Many would ask the question, how could this happen to Jimmy? He's a good guy who took care of his business, family, and was genuinely kind to others. He has a relationship with Jesus Christ and is a minister of the gospel who had been faithfully serving God. How could he go to war in Viet Nam, come back without a scratch, only to suffer in the manner that he was? However, Jimmy never did. He never complained and questioned God, why me? I tried to live as a child of God, served, and preached the gospel, how or why did this happen to me? No, his question was simply, "Why not me?" Trials and tribulations come to the righteous as well as the unrighteous and rains on the saint as well as the sinner. The scriptures tell us that all have sinned and come short of the glory of God and that the wages of sin is death. Well, that being true, all of us deserve death. For all of us have sinned, all of us have messed up and transgressed the Word of God, and deserve death, but God who is rich in mercy, has quickened us, that we shall live.

Freddie went to the hospital to check on Jimmy and was expecting to see hurt and pain, agony, despair, and possibly anger. However, when he got to the hospital, he was shocked to witness laughter, singing and praising God coming from his room. The Second New Hope Choir had shown up to pray and sing with him. It was then that Freddie had a deeper appreciation of the strength and faith of our older brother and how strong he really was. I have learned that many times, the trials of life that we encounter are not forms of punishment, but to the contrary that God, like Job has allowed us to go through a storm in life, not for ourselves but that others may be encouraged and strengthened to weather their personal trials. God allowed a particular storm in our life because He knew that you would be able to handle it, that you would be an encouragement to others to continue to fight the good fight. It is easier to have faith when everything is going your way. You have the gentle breeze of success at your back and the love and admiration of those in your corner, but what do you do when the storm of opposition is raging against you and trouble is on every hand? How do you react when you are faced with the uncertainty of tomorrow? It's not the trouble that has come your way is the question, but how you handle and deal with your adversity. How do you deal with hatred, racial bigotry, rape, unemployment, death, and sickness? For many of us, this becomes the new normal, and instead of fighting, we put on the robe of the victim and resolve that there's nothing that can be done to change the outcome of our circumstances.

My vantage point allows me to see an opportunity to excel in the face of defeat, that I am not a victim, but rather the victor. I can have victory in the face of defeat. I choose to believe that my God is not just a God when things are great, but He is also my God when the dark clouds hang low and friends are few. God has invested much in you and victory is in your DNA. We were wondrously made in His image and likeness and we have built into us the innate ability to imagine and create solutions when there may be no visible signs or resources available. This is your opportunity to excel, do or to become what God sees within you. That opportunity may present itself at work when your supervisor, for reasons good or bad, has placed you in predicament to become a victim, but you can use that opportunity to rise to the occasion and snatch victory from the jaws of defeat. They may have meant it to our detriment to be a victim, but God can use it to our good.

Romans 5:3-4 (KJV)

> And not only so, but we glory in tribulations also: knowing that tribulation worketh patience;
>
> And patience, experience; and experience, hope:

Paul reminds us that we can have the glory, understanding that the tribulation that we have to endure, is a process to strengthen our patience to be able to wait and be long suffering and our patience grants us the experience of our past to know that He is with us, and this experience brings that blessed hope. That hope to believe the unbelievable, to reach the unreachable, and to attain the unattainable. It is with this hope that will cause others to scratch their heads with disbelief that in spite of the odds against you, that you were able to claim the victory in Jesus name.

My father was the hardest working man that I have ever known. He worked hard at both jobs as well as being there for his family. He did not do a lot of socializing on the job, but was very social. It seems that he was trying to outwork his lack of education and the racial prejudices that he had to face on a daily basis. It was his opportunity to excel. On one occasion at the steel mill, his supervisors questioned his output of work for the day. They could not believe that one man did as much as my father's quota sheet indicated. He had single handedly produced more than the other two shifts combined. He was monitored on his next shift by his supervisors to inspect his quantity of work and Dad did as I have always known him to do, work hard. By the end of his shift, his supervisors came and apologized to him and remarked that they needed to keep closer tabs on the other shifts. He put this spirit of excellence in his children to work hard and use those opportunities as they arose, to excel.

I see people daily walking in defeat and a sense of hopelessness. They have given over to defeat before the battle has even begun. Those who were raised or perhaps visited the rural away from the city lights understand how dark it can get at night. It's so dark that it's difficult to see the ground around your feet. But if you can look up and see the vastness of the heavens as the stars light up the night sky, you can see the endless possibilities that are out there. Many times in life your opportunity to excel may be as simple as raising your head to see that there some options, some possibilities that are available to you that you will never see until you pick up your head. The Psalmist reminds us to keep our eyes to the hills from where come our help. Our help comes from the Lord. And as long as my help keeps coming from above, I continue to have hope, and with that hope comes possibilities to claim the victory in Jesus name.

Challenges in life, on your job or in your relationships are not punishments handed down, but depending on your vantage point, they can be excellent opportunities for you to stretch yourself past your comfort zone to do what you have never accomplished before. One accomplishment will lead to the second, and that second will lead to a pattern of an I can do it attitude. Take that next challenge not as an obstacle, but take the vantage point that this is your opportunity to excel. Understand that you are not the victim and you are not being punished but the victor that has yet to claim the prize.

HELP SOMEBODY

Your opportunity to excel may be as simple as helping someone else. Many times our view is restricted by personal obstacles on every side hindering our ability to see things as they really are and not as they may appear to be. It can be very easy to become overwhelmed by personal events, great and small that you can get disoriented in where your position really is and where your situation appears to have you. Unexpected events with our finances, families, health and world events can cause us to panic, and panic leads to an irrational thought process at the worst possible time, and those choices made under duress can have dire consequences and be even more costly physically, financially and mentally to fix. Sometimes we are so close to the issue that it become impossible to see it clearly. It becomes necessary to step back to get a good look and refocus on the whole picture and not that one detail that has you stuck. I have found it to be more true than not, that it's not as bad as it appears to be.

I've learned that taking the focus off of yourself for a while and focusing on someone else will often help you to better look at your own situations with a different perspective.

While traveling to Shreveport Louisiana on vacation during the summer of 1993, I was able to witness some of the damage caused by a flood that devastated the south as the people tried to pick up the pieces that had been so quickly swept away by nature. My heart went out to a people that I had never met before, and I had this burning desire to give some measure of help in some kind of way. And just like a fire, if there is nothing to fuel the flame, it will die out, and it was not long in my travel when that particular opportunity to help died without me doing a thing. It was about a year later that I was hired by the U.S. Army Corps of Engineers, and not knowing it at the time of applying for the job, they had in place a national emergency response program in place to give emergency assistance to those in need. God has afforded me a precious privilege to take the training by the Corps and give assistance and hope to various parts of the country that were in need. It's easier to give help and to show love to someone that you know, but there is a special reward on the inside that is gained when you stretch that helping hand to a stranger. I met some great people who were struggling to put their life back in order, some of great faith and others with none. There were those who had the resources to rebuild while others had nothing to rebuild with. They may have never acknowledged our efforts, said thank you or even knew that they were the benefactor of our efforts, but God gave Second New Hope a sense of peace and satisfaction in helping our brothers in their time of need. There is a special bond that was created by those men who left the comforts of their homes to minister. And every time I mention "Road Trip," the brothers line up to volunteer to help. God has given me a band of soldiers and an opportunity to excel by helping others that we would not have ever met if it were not for a tragic event in their lives.

Romans 12:1-2 (KJV)

> [1] *I beseech you therefore, brethren, by the mercies of God, that ye present your bodies a living sacrifice, holy, acceptable unto God, which is your reasonable service.*

² And be not conformed to this world: but be ye transformed by the renewing of your mind, that ye may prove what is that good, and acceptable, and perfect, will of God.

Paul pleads with us as believers in Jesus Christ to renew, to change our thought patterns, our mind set, our vantage point for a better point of view. A holy view, accepted through the lenses of God. When you change your mind set to the mind of Christ, your vantage point becomes more acute. Changes and necessary adjustments along the way are seen from a clearer and less obstructed view point that takes into account other potential challenges along the way.

When we present our bodies a living sacrifice unto God, we give Him the opportunity to use us in a way that sometimes maybe hard to articulate, but the experience and the feeling we get to be used in the service of God is incredible. That feeling reaches into our giving of our finances to fund the trip, our time needed, not just the trip, but also coordinating, sorting and folding clothes.

When the we as a people come together for a common purpose or cause and present our bodies to God as a living, willing and energetic sacrifice, great things can be accomplished. It does not take for one of us to give all, for Christ did that on Calvary, but when the body of Christ can all give some, on one accord, we can effect changes that often seemed impossible.

THE LITTLE CHURCH THAT COULD

My middle brother, Freddy, introduced our eldest brother, Jimmy, to a group of young people who would become not just friends, but family. They were David Thomas, who lived 2 blocks down and two sisters; Zanetta and Rhonda Gibson, who lived across 8 Mile Rd. in the Township. It was here that I found another benefit to living on Best Block USA, a refuge that would continue to reshape and refocus my vantage point. They invited Jimmy to attend their church in Royal Oak Township, Second New Hope Missionary Baptist Church, a small family church with a heart for God's people. At the time the church only had a basement to worship in. There was no large sanctuary with a balcony. There was no grand piano or larger than life pipe organ, just a piano that sat in the corner played by Ms. Bernice. The floor was not carpeted or even level, but every Sunday we had church. The choir was not the largest, there were no professional singers and no stars but just a few believers who still had a mind to live for Jesus, and they sang with the power of the Holy Spirit as if Jesus was sitting in the audience.

The pastor was Reverend Oddis Lewis Sr., a gray haired preacher from Arkansas with a 3rd grade education who appeared larger than life to me. He was a giant of a man who was unapologetic about his preaching and his love for Jesus Christ. His voice was so strong and piercing that he didn't need a microphone. He told young preachers not to worry about hearing the amens from the congregation, just preach the word. Pastor Lewis said something to me one Sunday between Sunday School and Morning Service when I was a young boy around 10 or 11. He put his hand on my shoulder and asked me how the young preacher was doing. I never thought much about him addressing me as a preacher because there were no thoughts or aspirations coming from me that desired to preach. It was not till I began my pastorate that his words came back to me and caused me to reflect on what my spiritual father was speaking into my life. Had God shown him something in me that one day I would be standing on the shoulders of his grandson, Pastor Gabriel Lewis, who would stand upon his? I was so close to the members there, that we were not like family, but we were family. His son, Pastor Alvin Lewis of the Family of God Baptist Church, was my Sunday School teacher and mentor. He took many of the teens to his house to play ping pong or to boxing matches. Mother Magdalene Andrews, the daughter of Pastor Oddis Lewis, reviewed the books of the bible with the entire Sunday School class. It was Mother Andrews who moved that I become the interim Pastor, after the resignation of Pastor Gabriel Lewis. It was these beautiful people along with the Mc littles', the Browns, Lewis, Parhams and so many more who were at Second New Hope to help shape the vantage point that I have now.

We remained in the basement a number of years and became known as the basement church. Although our worship was held in the basement, that did not define us as a church or our vantage point for kingdom building.

Many times we allow other's opinions, titles, and labels define us as a people, individuals or a nation and when you give others that authority over you, they now have the power to define who you are, and once others can define you they now have the power to confine you to a box of their expectations for you. Your hopes, dreams, and aspirations are nothing more than a dream.

When the conversation to expand and build came about, the question was asked how can we build when we don't have the finances? This was a legitimate issue that had to be addressed at some point in time if the church was ever going to grow beyond the basement. There were no affluent members who attended Second New Hope, just a handful of everyday, hardworking believers who were faithful.

Pastor Lewis' response was swift and to the point. We are not building on finance, but we are building on faith. Though few outside of us thought it was possible, we held on to all things are possible through Christ who strengthens us.

Doing anything through Christ requires us to examine our approach and align it with him. While dealing with this chapter, my pastor, called as he has been known to do and begin to teach/preach as he said whatever I do, make sure that it's not just good, but it's God. Many times we will get a thought that is an excellent idea that can have very positive results, but you need to also ask yourself the question; is it of God? Is it what God would have us to be doing and is it when we ought to be doing it? Just as it takes time for a fruit to ripen, there's a process that has to happen. A seed has to planted, germinate, take root, matured and be nurtured before it is ready to yield a harvest. Your good idea may be in the seed that has been planted into your spirit stage of its process and has not taken root, matures or even been nurtured yet to bear fruit.

Jesus was a good steward over all the resources that He had at His disposal. In the feeding of the multitude with two fish and five loaves of bread, several things happened. Jesus sent the disciples to assess what was available for the people to eat. The disciples came back with a negative report. They were only able to come up with two little fish and five loaves of bread to feed upwards of possibly five thousand men, women and children. The disciples put what they had into the hand of Jesus and He prayed to the great multiplier. He gave thanks to God before anything happened. It was not a prayer of hope, but Jesus showed us the power of prayer in earnest expectation. He prayed expecting God to answer it.

We cannot afford be blind or to ignore the honest reality of our personal lack of resources. The scripture plainly tell us to consider the cost before we build, that we do not become a mockery in the community. Acknowledge your lack, but likewise acknowledge the need and the source from where it comes. Financially, at Second New Hope there were no doctors, lawyers or engineers there to make large contributions to the building fund. There were just a small group of baptized believers who had limited financial resources to offer, who lived simple lives, but what they lacked in the way of finances they made up for in Faith, Prayer and a willingness to work. They took what they had and put it in the hands of the one who could do more with less. That little church kept the faith, gave what they could, and worked in the midst of the doubt and the snickering of others who could not see what was revealed to them and kept their eyes focused on the prize.

In 1970, three years after construction started, that basement church that nobody believed would ever leave the basement, and marched past the doubts, obstacles and snickering into a beautiful new sanctuary. Being one who was there in the basement and now worshiping upstairs is my constant reminder that although the opposition may be present and great, that the God that I serve is also there and much greater than any opposition past, present or any opposition that the future may bring. I have learned that being big does not necessarily equate to being better. Sometimes that thing that appears to be bigger is just swollen and needs to be elevated. Second New Hope is physically not a big church building in comparison to edifices that are being erected today. They are not a large church in comparison to the mega churches that are doing great works in Kingdom Building, but God has allowed a great work to flow from the Little Church that Could, when many doubted and railed against it to minister and let its little light to shine for all to see.

 David was the last and not even considered kingly material among his brothers by his own father, but was used by God, defeated a giant and became King of Israel. Gideon's family was the least of the tribe and he was the least of the family, yet God chose him to lead a small army to victory. Don't let your status, stature or vantage point established by others determine where your position or contribution in the world will be, but allow God to strategically place you where He would have you to be, to accomplish what His will is for you. And when you are in the right place at the right time, you will be better able to see what you are able to do, even when those around you cannot.

A VIEW FROM THE ROAD

Matthew 7:13-14 (KJV)

^{13} Enter ye in at the strait gate: for wide is the gate, and broad is the way, that leadeth to destruction, and many there be which go in thereat:

^{14} Because strait is the gate, and narrow is the way, which leadeth unto life, and few there be that find it.

    Living in the big city provides a person with almost endless possibilities to get from point A to point B. From my house I could take three different freeways to get to work, or I could stay off of the freeways and take the scenic route, or if time was not an issue, I could take side streets there. However, although there are many ways to get where you are going, not all routes are advantageous or desirable. Some roads may get you there faster but may require you to travel through a part of town that may not be safe. The direct route may be the most expedient way to travel, but there may be obstacles in the way due to an automobile accident. In time, your most used way of travel may have become worn and in need of repair that would delay your travel. Roads in the north are frequently in repair due to the harsh winter months that produce pot holes.

Harsh weather conditions may also cause one to alter travel plans to avoid slick spots and heavy traffic. Life on the road is filled with signs to lead in one direction or another.

Whichever way you decide to travel requires that you are aware of where you are and where it is that you are trying to go. When traveling out of state, I was always sure to get a map in order to plot the best way to get to our destination. As we travel this road called life, there are countless choices at our disposal to get where we are trying to go. Many times we are tempted to take shortcuts in order to hasten our trip, but not all ways of travel are the best way for you. The scriptures tell us that although a certain path may be available, that same path may lead to our destruction. Selling drugs for some is tempting because of the insane amount of money that you can make in a short amount of time. It looks like easy money and for some reason those who choose that road believe that they have a better plan that will make it where the others have failed. They chose to ignore the warning signs of slippery conditions, dead end, winding turns, and the victims they have left behind and history has proven that the road to success that seemed to be short, was not, and it led to either prison or to the local cemetery. Both are filled with individuals who thought they had the system beat. Jesus tells us that straight is the gate and narrow is the way to life and the other ways lead to our destruction. There is only one way to a right relationship with God and that is by Jesus. There's no other way, no short cut available that man may be saved, other than our Lord and Savior. He is the way, the truth and the life.

Life on the road is quick, fast, and adventurous, where everything is up close and personal and the smallest of distractions can be fatal. Life on the road does not afford you the luxury of seeing obstacles around the bend or knowing the condition of the very road that you're traveling.

I was riding with my son, talking about my call to the ministry where I shared with him some life applications that Pastor Lewis had shared with me. I told him that it was important for him as a child of God to watch all things. God can reveal things to you through things that you see everyday. As we were driving down the freeway, there was a tow truck stranded on the side of the road that was receiving assistance from another tow truck. He immediately asked, like that tow truck? Life on the road confirmed to the both of us that even those who give help to those in need may at some time need help themselves. Life on the road mandates that you look out for others. There will be those stranded on the side of the road who will be in need of your assistance, where there will be others to watch for who mean you no good. They are there to steal, kill or destroy.

Growing up in my family, traveling only meant traveling by car. I had never taken a train or flown by airplane until I was an adult. Traveling was fun because we usually went as a family with a minimum of two cars, usually, and sometimes as many as four. Road travel as a child could be exciting and adventurous. We learned to keep an eye out for one another. As technology got better, we had citizen band radios installed in our cars. This made it possible to keep track with one another, even though we had lost sight of one another. Now technology has grown and developed for those traveling by road too.

Colossians 3:1-3 King James Version (KJV)

[1] *If ye then be risen with Christ, seek those things which are*

above, where Christ sitteth on the right hand of God.

² Set your affection on things above, not on things on the earth.

³ For ye are dead, and your life is hid with Christ in God.

A view from the road is faster and immediate, but a view from above will take you further

Luke 9:61-62 King James Version (KJV)

⁶¹ And another also said, Lord, I will follow thee; but let me first go bid them farewell, which are at home at my house.

⁶² And Jesus said unto him, No man, having put his hand to the plough, and looking back, is fit for the kingdom of God.

Regardless of where you are driving to or from, there should always be two pieces of glass in front of you. They are not there for decoration but are there to aid and protect you as you travel. The largest glass is called a windshield. It's there to provide you with protection from the elements as well as to give you the widest view available. The windshield gives you a distinct vantage point to not only see those obstacles that may be in your direct path to allow you the ability to navigate around it, but it also allows you to be able to see potential threats approaching from your peripheral view, to adjust your speed to avoid a collision. The other piece of glass is considerably smaller than the windshield. The rearview mirror is there to allow the driver to keep looking forward while being able to see what's approaching from behind.

    Just as the windshield is much larger than the rearview mirror, we should be more focused on where we are headed to and less time on where we are leaving from. We stay stuck in the rearview mirror of our past. Our past mistakes, past failures and our past obstacles all have their place, and there should be some time for you to examine where you've been and what you learned to help you with where you are going, but it is not there for you to live in the past. I often hear my brother talk about the good ole days growing up in the 50s and 60s. Many times I reflect about my childhood growing up in the 60s and 70s, and to me those were the good ole days we love to romanticize, and to a kid they probably were the good ole days, but the truth of the matter is that those days were not all that good. As I spoke of in the introduction, there was so much unrest and so many leaders that we lost senselessly to the riots, war and drugs. We need to remember those days, learn from them and keep moving forward. If we spend too much time looking at what's behind us, with all of the twist and turns in the road that life has to offer us, in time we will end up off of the road and in a ditch because we were not focused on what's ahead of us. Many of the accidents that we encounter today are caused by distracted driving. Those who are operating the vehicle are simultaneously engaged in texting, eating or even applying makeup, and it only takes a moment of distraction to cause a fatal accident. I actually struggle with using the term, accident because an accident implies that something may have been unavoidable, but distracted driving is avoidable, yet we continue to do it.

    This road that we're traveling on called life has many twist and turns. Some will have signs posted to turn here for a short cut to the promise land. But there's no short cuts when it comes to where God will have you. There are some lessons that we need to learn, if not for not, but for later in the journey. There will be parts of the road that will be smooth sailing, whereas other parts are bumpy and filled with pot holes. There will be storms along the road, with slippery spots and debris to hinder your progress, but along the road you will see signs posted for your safety. Signs to tell you to slow down, and slippery when wet. Signs to let you know that the pavement is uneven or not safe to pass. My vantage point from the road is that constant reminder that they're obstacles, twists and turns happen, but It's these lessons that God has taught me early, that has sustained me this far.

THE CUTLASS CLUB

My parents gave me the down payment upon graduation to purchase a car to get back and forth to work, school and home. And the first car that I ever owned was a brand new 1977 Cutlass Supreme. Soon after that, one of my closest friends bought a 1976 Cutlass Supreme. And like most young men, we were heavy into our cars. From the sounds, wheels and accents to make it uniquely different. We worked and went to school together. When school was out; we rode, hung and partied together. We kept in touch with one another by CB radio. This was before cell phones. His handle was the Champion and mine was the Iceman. On one summer's day In 1979, as we were cruising the streets of Detroit, going nowhere in particular, we drove pass a bank parking lot on the Lodge Fwy Service drive and 6 Mile road, where there was a parking lot with only 1976-1977 Cutlass Supremes. We circled around and pulled up to see what was going on, only to meet some of the members of the Motor City Cutlass Club. Young men and women of different ages, professions and world views, who had similar interest in automobiles. It was not about a gang or underworld activity, just simply some young people who drove the same kind of car, who liked hanging together at the park and listening to loud music. There was no grass roots movement, political agenda or social causes to be championed, just young people hanging, I thought.

Somehow, I'm not sure how, but very quickly I became the president of the club. The membership kept growing and our name began spreading among the other car clubs and young people. Outside of the Corvette Club, who were in a different age and economic demographic, the Cutlass Club was the largest in the City of Detroit. We became local celebrities. Kids would holler out Ice, as I pass them by. With my new position and newly found fame, I begin to look at the club as no longer just young people hanging out, but young adults with a voice and a responsibility in the community and the agenda began to shift from hanging to making a change as we hung. On one occasion as I was waiting at Palmer Park for some of the other guys to gather, when a police officer asked if I had a moment to talk. I got in the front seat of the police car and the officer was genuinely sharing his concern with our driving, blocking traffic and causing congestion as we moved from one park to another. And as the officer was talking to me, people unafraid of the police, some not attached to the club, approached the squad car, knocked on the window and asked if I was okay? And I quickly **responded that everything was cool. And the officer looked at me with a look that asked, who is this guy? And then it hit me, that I was a part of something bigger than some kids hanging out at the park.**

   Detroit being a Democratic city; I started hanging around a group of young Democrats who knew the workings of the political machine and who was operating it. And as much as I was interested in them, it appeared that they were interested in us, for they seen a potential gold mine of untapped voters. The 13th Congressional District invited me to attend meetings and soon made their office on Dexter Ave available for the Cutlass Club to use on occasion for meetings and a couple of parties. I became the face of the Cutlass Club and they assigned some seasoned young Dems to teach and guide us as we moved into uncharted waters. Many of us did not have much, other than our cars. We were raw, street kids, unlearned to politics and big business and I had just enough of both worlds to be dangerous. But I was a quick study and knew when to shut up and listen. As I attended a young dems meeting, a young man stood and made the strangest statement. He stood and boldly announced that he did not like the way things were developing and he did not care who the Cutlass Club was! I had no idea what his statement meant or what in the world he was talking about. The few of the club members who were in attendance looked at one another with confusion as to what was going on. Ray, who was one of the advisors assigned to guide us, quickly took me outside to talk to me. I asked him, what was going on? He answered and revealed to me that there has been a lot of conversation about the potential of the club and that this conversation found its way to Washington and this made some of the established young Dems uncomfortable with their position in the political picture of politics.

My vantage point was growing and expanding exponentially. I was seeing more and beginning to understand the potential that others were seeing in the Cutlass Club. Depending on the vantage point, others will see potential in you that you never realized existed and depending on their agenda, they may try to exploit it for their benefit, eradicate it or to develop it to become all that it can be. I told Ray that we were there to help and that we didn't have time for mess, but he assured me that everything was good and that young man was just being insecure. It was soon after that incident that I began getting invitations to different social events. They, whoever they are, gave me tickets to see a Tommy Hearns fight and to a party. I asked Cameo Bill if he wanted to go to the fight. These were not ordinary tickets. As we stood in line to get into Joe Louis Arena, the ticket taker was rude as he was shouting at those waiting to get in, to have their tickets out. When he got to me and seen the tickets, he paused, looked at me, turned and signaled to an usher, who promptly addressed us as sir and escorted us to our box to see the fight. Wow! We found ourselves in another world, surrounded by aliens. We were leather jackets and gym shoes and they were wearing fur coats, diamonds and sipping champagne. Once again, we were being exposed to a vantage point of greater potential. Politicians and would be politicians were inviting me to more events while introducing me to their daughters and nieces, trying to get my endorsement.

Unrestrained power is dangerous. I began believing the hype that somehow I had real power. I began devising a plan to reach out to all of the car clubs and unite them, further expanding our base of influence. I felt that we could collectively drive down the price of gas by targeting certain chains at a time, by boycotting those while buying from the others could force them to lower their prices. I discussed this plan with my father in our kitchen and it concerned him to no end. He told me that they would kill me messing around with their money, but I had the fever. That fever that can come with power, real or perceived. I had it and I was not afraid. I thought about King and his willing to die for what he believed. In our life, there has to be something that we believe in that we are willing to stand and yes, possibly fall for. Our faith, family, country or a cause to right that thing that maybe wrong. I had a great relationship with my father and trusted his opinion and learned to listen to him and decided that the price of gas was not the cause, yet that fire kept burning in me to provoke change. It has been said that fame is fleeting, for it's here today and it will be gone tomorrow. For two years the Cutlass Club hung out at the park, attended parties and did what young adults did. We begin to grow up, find other interest, relationships and soon the car club and any political aspirations faded into memories. But during that time, I met some awesome people who God used to help shape and to hone who I was, who I was becoming, and the outlook for the future of my vantage point. People who saw something in me that I had not fully recognized in myself. People with different backgrounds socially, educationally and economically were drawn to me to pour into a kid who drove an Ice Blue Cutlass Supreme who was able to connect with other people.

    Rising up in certain circles does not necessarily equate to possessing a better vantage point. I experienced vantage points that lacked stability, clarity, substance or longevity. There was a Hebrew baby by the name of Moses, who was set adrift by his mother to save him, only to drawn out by the sister of Pharaoh. Moses was raised in the palace of Pharaoh, with all of the conveniences and trappings that came with it. He received the best of education, food, clothes and the riches, but life at that perceived elevation did not give him the clarity of God's purpose for his life. It only served to shape his skills needed along with the lessons he received on the backside of a mountain, tending sheep, to lead a nation to the promised land.

RISE UP AND BUILD

In the summer of 2001, an email at my job was sent out to the emergency responders looking for volunteers to deploy to West Virginia to give aid to the flood victims there. I flew into the Huntington West Virginia airport. As I departed the airport in my rental car, I could read on their license plates: wild and wonderful. And it truly was. They had some of the prettiest countryside that you'll ever want to see, with some of the tallest and thickest trees and huge majestic mountains everywhere you look, with meandering streams along the foot of those mountains. Winding around those mountains were narrow two lane highways that took you from one small town to another. It looked like a Norman Rockwell painting, and it was as pretty as a postcard could be.

However I've learned early in life that all is not always as it appears to be. As a matter of fact, your neighbor's grass may look greener on their side of the fence, but if you look a little closer, you may find that their grass has a lot of brown spots in it also. Oh, it looks good from a distance, but if you can take a little peek from a closer proximity, you may get a different story.

West Virginia is situated among mountains. Small communities were built in the low places between the mountains, that we call valleys, but the locals called them hollars. And yes, the mountains were beautiful and majestic, but down in those hollars, life painted a different picture. Entire towns have been devastated and destroyed by floods that followed the heavy rain that fell the night before. I saw entire towns that had been wiped out in a matter of hours. Their homes, clothes, possessions, food, and many jobs were gone. You could visibly see months later how high the water had risen by where their clothes had got stuck in the trees, up over their heads.

    I went to West Virginia believing that I was going to be a blessing to some people who were in need, and they were in need. The truth of the matter was that they blessed me more than I ever thought possible, and I believed that I left with far more than I brought. Those people had a dogged determination that with God they were gonna make it, and one by one the local citizens told their stories of where they were and what happened to them. This one town in Wyoming County in particular had 61 businesses. Out of those 61 businesses, 60 of them were damaged by the flood, but instead of throwing in the towel and surrendering to the devastation that had found its way on their doorstep, the store owners wrote words of encouragement on their buildings that said, "We will return," and "Tough times don't last forever, but tough people do," and "We shall overcome."

    Through all of the mess and destruction, there was one store window that stuck with me more than all the others. I was with a contractor going to survey the next sight, and while leaving that town, heading to the next, I read in the window, "Rise up and build." and Neh 3:16 at the bottom. Those four words leaped in my spirit. I couldn't wait to get back to that store to confirm what my eyes had seen, but when I returned a half hour later, the sign was gone. When I got back to my hotel room later that evening, I went to my bible to verify what I had seen in that town. It was the story of Nehemiah and the task given him by God to rebuild the walls at Jerusalem.

Nehemiah 2:18

> *¹⁸ Then I told them of the hand of my God which was good upon me; as also the king's words that he had spoken unto me. And they said, Let us rise up and build. So they strengthened their hands for this good work.*

To accomplish this task, Nehemiah would face opposition, distractions, accusations and threats to prevent him from completing the task that he was anointed to do. That required him to have a particular vantage point above his enemies. I believe in my heart that God left that message for me to see and take this vantage point to his children, that no matter where you're at in life, no matter what your trouble struggles and trials, that you can rise up and build.

Nehemiah was the cup bearer to the Persian King Artaxerxes. To be the cup bearer required of you to be trusted, for you literally held their lives in your hands. The cup bearer not only brought the cup to the king, but he would also taste the contents of the cup for poison. To hold such a position of importance meant that the king had the utmost confidence and trust in Nehemiah. This level of trust that the king held for him was a reflection of Nehemiah's integrity. What makes Nehemiah's position with the king so interesting is that Nehemiah was in bondage and the king entrusted his life to a man who was taken away from his home to serve the whims and desires of an enemy. Because of his trust and admiration, the king gave Nehemiah permission and the financing to go to Jerusalem and rebuild the walls that had been destroyed. A better vantage point requires us to walk with integrity regardless of our surroundings and circumstances.

Upon arriving at Jerusalem with his mission, Nehemiah went out at night to inspect the walls and determine the level of work that was needed. During the day, there were those who would be overwhelmed by the amount of damage and the work necessary to repair it and their ability to repair it. Nehemiah went out at night to avoid the distractions and the naysayers, to best determine a plan of action. In 2009, during the nation's housing crisis, I bought a fixer upper, a beautiful, three bedroom ranch that sat on a ½ acre lot. I took my brother by to see my future home and the first thing out of his mouth was, "could I get my money back?" He was looking at what the house was and I seen it's potential, for the home that it would become. Your vantage point is dependent on you getting away from all of the negative voices and influences that will sabotage or obscure your view, in order to clearly see what's in front of you. The scriptures tell us plainly to pray, seek wise counsel and to consider the cost before we build and I did all of that. I made my request known to God, I had an inspector to certify that the house was sound, a contractor to tell me how much the project was going to cost and I was fully aware of the finances that I had available to spend. There will people who may be in your inner circle who cannot see the vision that is within you. As a mother pregnant with child has to take precautions to protect her unborn baby, we have to be careful to protect that vision that is growing in us.

In his rage towards Nehemiah for rebuilding the wall, Sanballat ask the question, will the Jews fortify themselves and sacrifice to complete the wall? This is a question that we all must answer at one time or another. Are we ready to fortify ourselves? As we rebuild our personal walls, we must not be content to simply throw up a wall, but to erect a wall that has been fortified, reinforced and strengthened to endure not only the battles today, but those battles that are sure to come in the future. We fortify ourselves daily by our devotion to God, to pray and seek His will in our lives, to be faithful in our commitment to ministry, and our attendance to worship services. All of this nourishes our spiritual resolve to build regardless of the opposition before us. This build may require you to make sacrifices that others may not see, understand and possibly resent. Sacrifices in your finances and your time may be needed to complete your wall. As you walk the path that is set before you, you will encounter those standing around, doing nothing but criticizing, raising doubts, and opposition, when they could be a part of the solution, rather than a part of the problem. Not everyone is blessed with the clarity of a better vantage point that you may have, to see not only what you see, but how to get there from where you are.

Your mission to rise up and build also requires your focus to be on the mission before you. There will be obstacles and distractions coming from various directions. Distractions that will slow down and hinder your progress. Nehemiah encountered accusations, whispers, and lies to get him to stop his work and come down and address them, but he stayed focused and asked why should he come down, when he has work to do? To obtain that better vantage point, we must pray, have integrity, fortify ourselves and stay focused, to see the prize.

SELLING UMBRELLAS

 To ask a question may be considered a strange way to begin a chapter in a book, but I believe that it's necessary to help you to attain a vantage point better than the one that you presently possess, right now. You may have a fairly good vantage point or even a great one, but just maybe, this will help you achieve a better outlook or path to your future or merely confirm that where you are is it.

 Do you have an umbrella, and can you put your hands on it when you need it? I personally have a large umbrella in my car, and I also keep a smaller one in my briefcase. I believe most families have at least one umbrella, but the problem too often is when you need it, you cannot locate it, or it's not large enough to cover the entire family during the storm. By design, an umbrella is a portable instrument or apparatus used by individuals to provide them with a limited amount of protection from the rain. Some umbrellas are large enough to give protection to two individuals, whereas some umbrellas are compact in size to protect only one.

 I have seen umbrellas used in ways other than keeping you dry from the rain. Some use umbrellas when there is not a drop of rain to be found or a cloud in the sky. As a matter of fact, the sun is high and bright, we may use that instrument to provide us with shade from the intense heat from the sun. Umbrellas are also used to provide its users with support and stability while walking.

We were created in the image and likeness of God and by heredity have the innate ability to create. We have within us the ability to create umbrellas as protection not from only protection the storms, but God has also given us what we need to provide us with stability in shaky and unstable times. That gift from God has been a provider of shade and comfort even during times when things are good. The problem with too many of us is that we have put away that umbrella and cannot recall where we put it. What is that gift inside of you that is needed to shelter you through the storm or to provide you with stability when there's none apparent? Your umbrella may simply be your ability to cook or sew. It may be that gift that you have learned through the years and that you've placed on a shelf and forgotten about. Lawn care, house cleaning, or snow removal. I was having a conversation with a friend who told me that he had to go because there was some money on the ground and he had to go and pick it up. I looked at him strangely as he opened the door as I saw that it was snowing outside. I laughed, understanding what he was talking about. The next time I saw him, he told me that he made $300.00 dollars that night. $300.00 dollars that he did not have and $300.00 to provide him with some protection when the next financial storm comes, and trust me, it is coming. I met a young man at the gym who had a regular job, but also made $60,000.00 in one season, pushing snow. His umbrella provided him with $60,000.00 extra dollars, which is more than the average American makes in a year.

My wife Odetta's umbrella was providing daycare for twenty plus years. Her umbrella provided the family with the stability to pay down our debt, send our son to private school and take several trips to Georgia every year.

That umbrella will provide you with gap insurance when things break down, and things will break down, usually at the worst possible time. Many of us will find ourselves caught in a storm without that protection that an umbrella provides. A study reported that 30% of Michiganders could not put their hands on $500.⁰⁰ in an emergency. That means that if the hot water tank goes or your car needs to be repaired, that 3 out of 10 of us do not have the finances to get it fixed. That number rises to 70% for those needing a $1,000.⁰⁰. That umbrella that you've laid aside and can't find is that tool that you need to fill that gap in case of emergency and to weather your storm or possibly someone else close to you.

While on vacation, I was lounging by the pool. The sun was high and bright, so I opened the poolside umbrella to give me some shade. That umbrella will also provide you with some comfort. You're able to go and to do things, but that umbrella may provide you with a little cushion to stay a little longer on that trip or to stay at a nicer hotel. Early in our marriage we took a trip to Daytona Beach, Florida. We could barely afford to go, but we went. We had to stay in an extremely low-end motel and could not afford to go to the nicer restaurants. But now we can afford to fly, stay at 4 Star hotels, and dine at the finer restaurants because we had umbrellas in place to provide us with shade, even when times are good.

There's another umbrella that many have laid aside and cannot remember where, called stewardship. As a whole, we spend money that we don't have, trying to keep pace with other people trying keep pace with this family called the Jones's. Everyone is trying to keep up to prove that they have something that they don't really have. Actually, many of us earn enough to live, but we borrow and borrow and pay 25-30% interest rates to send them to far away destinations while we stay behind and finance their fun.

You may be in a position that you 're not sure what or where your umbrella is. You may have even convinced yourself that you don't have a gift that's needed. Stop it! I heard of one young man who earned $100,000.^{00} in a year cleaning windows and of others who make $500.^{00} in a weekend driving for Uber. You've allowed the enemy to convince you that you're hopelessly stuck and can't get out of it. The devil is a lie, but you have to want it for yourself! You may only need your umbrella temporarily. Take it out, open it up as needed, and tuck it away after the storm has passed. Make sure to put it where you can find it. You may choose to make a career out of it or only deploy your umbrella to pay for a vacation.

Our better vantage point may simply be blocked by finances or the lack thereof. Solomon says that money answers all. Whatever your umbrella maybe, find it. Search the house, garage, or the car to find that thing that you possess, to give you that protection you need, when you need it, and as often as you need it.

A VIEW FROM THE MOUNTAIN TOP

  Viewing life from the road gives you an immediate and close up perspective of your vantage point; however many times your perspective is limited or incomplete. To get a better vantage point of your surroundings requires that you rise above where you are to see where you've been in relation to where you are, but more importantly, to see where you are headed. Odetta and I traveled to the San Jacinto Mountains in Palm Springs, California. In Palm Springs, the temperature was above 100 degrees every day of the trip. It was hot and dry. There was the noise and congestion that accompanies any city, much more in larger cities.

  While we were there, many of the locals told us that we really needed to take the tram up the mountain to see the view from above. We took their advice and took the tram ride nearly 2 ½ miles up to the peak of the mountain, and the view did not disappoint. It was absolutely beautiful. We were able to see the landscape and mountain ranges from nearly 200 miles away. However, besides the obvious expectation, there were some unexpected experiences in our rise to the mountain top. While the temperature down in the valley was above 100 degrees. the higher elevation on the mountain was a comfortable 40 degrees cooler, and where the landscape in the valley consisted mostly of desert sand and cactus, there was green everywhere we turned. Beautiful trees that could not survive the harsher conditions below are thriving in the higher elevations. Not only was it more comfortable and colorful, but it was also noticeably quieter. There was a real sense of peace and tranquility that showed on the faces of the people as they hiked along the trails or just sat and took in the view around them. There was no hustle, no bustle, no congestion or city chaos, just calm and quiet.

When I think about the harsh realities that life will often present, with the overwhelming heat of a frustrated people, whether racial issues, financial, employment or the lack of employment, continued gang, and drug activities or terrorist issues that now seem to face us daily, societal life can have a temperature reach a boiling point. Things that seemed to happen naturally around me growing up and took for granted on Best Block USA are now seemingly lying dormant, or even worse, drying up and dying. Relationships in the community, in the neighborhood, and even within the walls of our own homes are dry and barren. Playgrounds that used to be alive and vibrant, now lay barren and desolate. Homes that were alive with families and beautifully kept lawns are now nothing more than shells of houses that are empty of the very things that made it a home, such as love, joy, prayer, and togetherness. These homes are waiting for the sticker that says that this structure is not safe for occupancy and has been condemned. Although homes were often filled with chaos and confusion that comes with having children in the house, there was a controlled sense of chaos by Mom and Dad, not by babies left to raise themselves while being entertained by what was on television.

The home that I speak about was not a result of a moving to a more affluent neighborhood due to a rise in the parent's, personal income. There were many people who made substantially more money, but did not live in a home, but the home was created on purpose. It was no mistake. It was the result of a deliberate and purposeful action by parents who raised up the expectations of the whole. Parents went to the mountain top where they could see where they came from, where they were, and what was needed to get where they were trying to go. When the family is elevated to more favorable environmental conditions, the offspring can grow in a greenhouse with fertile soil and constant care and grow stronger regardless of how barren the conditions are on the outside of the home. When the home is elevated, the noise, chaos and confusion on the outside is lessened to levels that allow those on the inside to see, hear, and digest what the rest of the world cannot see, hear, or even understand. There were many sounds in my neighborhood that were not heard, or if they were heard, were weeded out and discarded off of the elevated street called Best Block. There were certain expectations and behaviors in place there for the parents as well as the children.

    Please do not misunderstand that I want the world to believe that we were perfect or lived in a bubble. Our parents were not perfect, and we definitely were not perfect, but there was always that sense of what was acceptable back home. There was an elevated bar, and those things that did not rise up to that standard were kept elsewhere. It is those who were exposed to a view from the mountain top who dared to walk higher, expect higher, and to desire more out of life, have a code rooted into our nature to rise up and do.

    A home is definitely a house, but a house is not necessarily a home, and to take a view from the mountain top is more work than I can put together in a few sentences. When I went to that mountain top in Palm Springs, I paid a fare and rode a tram. In the matter of a few minutes, I was there looking at the beauty that I was expecting.

However, rising to the mountain top experience in life is filled with challenges, obstacles, and opposition.

I have so much love and admiration for Martin Luther King, Jr. My grandmother called him, her little Joseph, in reference to the Joseph in the Holy scriptures who would, after many trials and tribulations, rise up to bring his family to Egypt and save that nation and the nation of Israel, yet to be born during the famine. My admiration for Dr. King came perhaps more after his death than before, because on that day, April 4, 1968, I was a young 9 year old boy who did not fully appreciate or understood the struggles of my people of color. On that evening I was at a cub scout meeting. Without explanation, we were told to go straight home. It was not till I got home that I learned that Dr. King had been assassinated on a hotel balcony in Memphis, Tennessee. It was then that I begin to hear more about him in his dying than I did in his living. I saw adults crying out of hurt and frustration. I saw the tanks back on the streets again almost a year later for fear of another riot.

Radio stations began airing his speeches. Televisions began showing documentaries and biopics of the dreamer. Men, women, boys and girls, white and blacks would recite the words of the Dreamer. His most famous speech, "I Have A Dream," pricked the heart and conscience of a nation to become more than we were and that one day we would be a people not judged by the color of our skin but by the content of our character. His speech that resonated so deeply into my spirit was his "I've been to the Mountaintop Speech." It was this speech, his last speech that he gave on the eve of his assassination that I go to most. It is this speech that encourages me to keep climbing. He spoke so eloquently about his trials and tribulations along his journey. He spoke about the accomplishments and accolades that he had received along the way and the attempts that had been made on his life. However, he said that he's not fearing any man for he has been to the mountain top and God has allowed him to see the promised land. He told us that he may not get there with us, but we as a people will get to the promised land.

I hear people talk about their hopes, dreams, and aspirations for the future as they make their way to their promised land, but for too many, I have failed to see or hear about their climb up the rough side of the mountain. We want the promise, are looking for the promise, and expecting the promise, but too many of us are not ready to climb up the rough side of the mountain to see the promise awaiting.

We want to name it and claim it, grab it and blab, and call it and haul it, but nobody wants to climb. We don't want to work, struggle, or strain to achieve. We'd rather sit, wait, and receive it. Our strength comes out of the struggle. Our strength is developed during the storms of life and not the pleasant sunshiny days and gentle breeze of success at your back, but it comes when you have to dig deep and reach against all opposition, keeping your eyes on the prize of the high calling.

Philippians 3:13-15 King James Version (KJV)

> [13] *Brethren, I count not myself to have apprehended: but this one thing I do, forgetting those things which are behind, and reaching forth unto those things which are before,*
>
> [14] *I press toward the mark for the prize of the high calling of God in Christ Jesus.*

Paul says that he presses for the mark. He may fall short sometimes, but he presses for the mark of the prize.

My view from the mountain top happened February 1996. It was early into my calling as a minister of the gospel of Jesus Christ. I was attending a ministers conference hosted by the Georgia State Baptist Convention. It's an annual event where pastors and preachers from all over the state of Georgia come together to sharpen our tools, recharge our spiritual batteries, fellowship and encourage one another to continue to fight the good fight of faith. The conference was held on a forty-acre piece of property owned by the Baptist Convention. This particular property was once owned by a slave master, where the home had been restored and used for class rooms. There was a slave shanti next to it, roped off for visitors to see. During the civil war, this property became a hospital for the Union Army. In the mid 1900s, it became a shelter for unwed mothers and in the late 1980s the Georgia Baptist purchased the property to use to help rehabilitate those addicted to drugs. This property was located in rural Georgia, between Atlanta and Macon, isolated from the noise and chaos that comes from the big city and from the trappings that have at one time or another distracted most of us. They built Barack's style dorms to accommodate the visitors where four men shared a room and two rooms shared a bathroom. This forty-acre piece of property that has come to mean so much to me was located on a mountain top. We had to drive along a two lane, winding, blacktop roads, which led to a red dirt road that was often slick and muddy from the storms. There was no room service, only one phone line and no fancy wake up calls from the front desk. Instead, we were awakened every morning by one of the brothers singing one of those old call and response hymns that has brought us so far. There was no keyboard, drums, or even a tambourine to play the music. The words simply flowed so strongly from his heart, and it sounded something like A Charge to keep I have, and a God to Glorify. One by one other brothers would join in the wakeup call. It's this place that was so far removed from everything that I journeyed nearly 800 miles to get to, and it was worth every minute that it took me to reach.

There were preachers from varied backgrounds and levels of education, from those holding their doctorate to those who had their high school diploma and, to some who may not have completed school at all. Some arrived in a Mercedes Benz while others drove an old pickup. Some wore finely tailored suits while some were comfortable in their overalls. Some came from large congregations and others from small ones, but all assembled themselves together with the singular commonality of preaching the Word of God.

On this one particular night, the spirits were high as the Word of God went forth. In between sessions we took a short break. I walked out of the chapel and saw the vastness of God as I looked through the darkness of the night to see the skies lit up with stars for as far as I could see. It was on that mountain that I realized for myself how insignificant and tiny my world was, yet so significant that God continues to take the time to maintain and sustain it.

It was at that point on that mountain that a conference for men was placed into my spirit, and I said to myself out loud that we need this in Detroit. I was only an associate and eight years from being the pastor of Second New Hope. I did not know how and I did not know when, but I felt that the Men of God needed a place to gather, come apart from the distractions of life's everyday hassles, and to strengthen one another as we hear from God that we may be able to go back down into the valley that we left behind. We do not come to the mountaintop to stay, although many times it is the sentiment to stay in this happy place. However, the work and those depending on us are back in the valley, and it's that mountaintop experience that has equipped us to be the men that God has called us to be: better husbands, better fathers, better friends, and better leaders in the community, so we can make a difference and leave this a better place to be.

 I tucked away what the Lord revealed to me and only shared it with a few people. I've learned that you cannot share everything with everybody. Not everyone wants men to rise up and be where we were called. I stored it away what had been given while attending other conferences. Some were Christian and others for work. I watched and learned what worked and what did not. I observed the agendas, the cost, and the venues, for there would come a time to give birth to that seed that was in me. In May of 2004 Pastor Lewis unexpectedly stepped down as our pastor, and I became the third pastor of the Second New Hope Missionary Baptist Church. In November of that same year, we hosted our first revival under my pastorate where Pastor Branch gave me those words to Walk in My Authority. I soon started a new ministry called the Chosen Men of Standard. It was a ministry to challenge and encourage men to rise up and raise the standard of a world that was lowered by apathy, inactivity, laziness, and a lack of motivation. Growing up, my friends and I used to hang out all the time. We had a great time being together, but men of the church seem to have grown comfortable with isolating themselves from the whole. We seldom hang around to fellowship, and few make an effort to get together with the body of Christ outside of the walls of the church building. I purposely begin creating opportunities for the men of Second New Hope to come together as brothers and friends. I begin exposing our men to other brothers from other churches with fellowship opportunities. We begin attending other conferences, and who would have guessed that men of God still like eating, fishing, bowling, and watching sports on television? We have a group of men who now understand that they are a part of something greater than themselves and have realized and embraced the conviction that, "I am my brother's keeper." The Chosen Men of Standard have raised the standard to have the back of his brothers and sisters, to be there in their time of need, and not just in those times when all is well.

I begin planning and strategizing a men's conference, searching for a theme, the right speakers, an agenda, and the right venue far enough from Detroit to get away, yet close enough to get back home in case of an emergency. In the fall of 2005, I was invited by Pastor James Minnick of the Mt. Pleasant Baptist Church to attend a weekend getaway with him and his men. It was called "Hanging with My Brothers." Pastor Minnick and I, along with our good friend, Reverend Earl Tate, whom the Lord has called home to Glory, were all ordained together. Pastor Minnick had been called to pastor five years before my calling. He is progressive, articulate, and cool under pressure. He has a heart for the men of God to rise up within the body of Christ, and I felt comfortable in calling him my Big Brother. He understood the traditional church and the associated groups and organizations attached to it, an area where I was lacking. Pastor Minnick likewise had a men's ministry called the Mighty Men of Mount Pleasant who also marched to the beat of a different drum. I accepted his invitation to hang with the Brothers, and I got two of my associates to ride with me, Reverend Harris and Williamson, so they could watch and learn.

We took that 1 ½ hour drive north of Detroit to Midland, Michigan. The hotel was perfect. There was a bowling alley, restaurant, and arcade across the parking lot for fellowship. I had found my venue and my first speaker: Pastor Minnick. I called Pastor Lewis in Orlando, Florida to see if he was available, and he was. I called my childhood friend, Reverend Dr. Craig Ester of New Prospect Baptist Church, who grew up with me on Best Block, USA, Pastor Jake Gaines of Synagogue Baptist Church, Haman Cross of Rosedale Park, and Brother Ellis Liddell of ELE Wealth Financial Management. I had my lineup. I wanted to deal with the Spiritual, the Financial, and the Physical aspects of our lives to raise up that group of men who had the audacity to proclaim Christ! I called it the Chosen Men of Standard Mountaintop Conference.

In May of 2006 we opened up the doors to the Mountaintop Conference and watched seventy men walk in to what God had shown me ten years before in a vision as I stood on a mountaintop in Georgia. Many times the Lord will not move until we show the faith to move towards Him. Moses saw the burning bush, but God did not speak to him until he moved. Too many of the children of God have had a special seed planted into their spirit to minister or make a change in their lives but have not moved toward the promise that has been revealed. Climb your mountain. Your mountain may be steep, and it may be rough and rugged, but climb your mountain. Your mountain maybe treacherous, tricky, and tiring, but climb your mountain. The mountain that God has for you, is for you, and many times you may tell yourself that you cannot reach the summit, but keep on climbing. Your strength is being developed and forged as you struggle and strain to give birth to what others could not conceive. Focus on the next cliff or the next crevice or ledge to grab hold. Remind yourself of what you are doing, why you are doing it, and who gave it to you to do it because there will be times when there's no one around to remind you of the reason for making this climb. When you ascend to the top, stand on the summit and see what the Lord has allowed you to do regardless of all of the evidence that said that it could not be done. You will realize that all things are possible through Christ who strengthens you, preparing you for the next climb a little higher to the next assignment. Standing on the peak of the mountaintop can be a lonely place, but there's also clarity to see further and peace to hear that quiet, still voice telling you of a job well done, to take it in, and to move on to the next climb.

LEAVE IT ON THE FIELD

I love sports. On Best Block USA, we played most sports growing up. From baseball to basketball to football, we played it. We played in the gym, and we played on the street. We played organized little league, we played against other streets in the neighborhood, and we played against each other. We played till the street lights came on, and that was our signal that the game was over.

We were competitive. It could've been shooting pool, playing ping pong till 2 o'clock in the morning, or just shooting marbles in the dirt. We competed. Looking back over the years, a long way from Best Block USA, it was that competitive spirit among friends that gave us that edge in life. Regardless of what career path we took or how far we matriculated in school, we carried that spirit of teamwork and competition with us.

It did not matter how good or how bad the team appeared. I believed that we had a chance to win. Many times I took the weaker team with the belief that we could win. Attitude, teamwork, and experience can turn what is good to something great. A great coach has the ability to bring the best out of a team, to sometimes do what they did not know they were capable of doing.

In the 2006 NBA finals, the Detroit Pistons were matched up against the Los Angeles Lakers. Detroit was a team without a superstar. They were a blue collar, gritty, unified, attitude-filled group of men going up against a starting five, hall of fame dream team. There was no one outside of Detroit that gave the Pistons a chance in the world to beat the Lakers.

Those Pistons were on the Lakers like they stole something. They were a fine-tuned machine, straight out of a Motor City assembly line. Every piece fit together and complimented the whole. Those Pistons did the improbable by beating the Lakers in five games. They let game four get away in the final seconds of the game. It should've been in four.

Strangely enough, as much as I love sports, I don't like to watch it much, especially if it is one of my favorite teams playing. I believe in part because, being as competitive as I am and wanting to win, there's nothing I can do to change the outcome of the game by watching. Too many in life want to play the spectator, and although there is some satisfaction in seeing and celebrating your team winning, there is nothing you can do to change the outcome of the game. To make a difference, you have to be in it to win it.

Too many are content to live life as a spectator and let life happen. It's easy to live life as an armchair quarterback from the safety of your living room, second-guessing those that are in the spotlight, taking a swing at their spot in history.

When NBA great Michael Jordan was playing with the Chicago Bulls and the game was on the line, everyone knew who was getting the ball. The other team knew it, the referees knew it, and everyone in the stands knew it. Mike was getting the ball. Win or lose, Mike wanted the ball.

I never liked losing. Being the competitor, losing left a bad taste in my mouth. But the reality is in this life, no matter how good you may be, losses come. And I can accept losing a game if my teammates and I gave it our all. Sometimes as much as we want to win, our all is not good enough, but If I have to lose, let me be the one at the foul line or standing in the batter's box. When I played ball with my son Eric, I never just let him win. I made him earn it.

2 Timothy 4:7 (KJV)

> *[7] I have fought a good fight, I have finished my course, I have kept the faith:*

The apostle Paul in his letter to Timothy says that he has been in battle, where he won some and he lost some. There were times when the odds were against him, times when it appeared that he had no chance of getting the victory, but Paul said that regardless the odds and no matter how bleak the appearance, he fought the good fight. He said he was beat, stoned, jailed and shipwrecked, but he fought the good fight. Regardless of the obstacles and opposition, he fought the good fight. He did not waver, or compromise, but he fought the good fight and finished his course. All did not receive Jesus as their Lord and Savior, but he did what was assigned for him to do. Paul finished his assignment, and he kept the faith.

And because Paul did all that he could do, by preaching and teaching and living the life before man that he was proclaiming, he was able to boldly proclaim that he had no regrets.

Do you have any regrets? Did you give it your all, or did you half-step your way through your journey? We are living in a day and time of the half-step. We half-step at school, half-step at work, half-step at home, and we half-step at church, and then we wonder and complain when we half-make it. We somehow feel that just because we showed up, we are somehow entitled to it all. Not too many want to struggle or strain for a purpose or cause. They just want to receive the reward. They don't want to climb the rough side of the mountain. They just want to see the promised land, but in the reward and within the promised land is a process where there are challenges and obstacles, struggles and some strains we need to overcome to claim the promise.

Growing up there was a term used that said, "Woulda-Coulda-Shoulda." You would have, could have, or should have done any number of things, but there was always one excuse after another not to do it. "Woulda-Coulda-Shoulda." The world is full of reasons and excuses to postpone, delay, or abort your dream, and many of them have a hint of validity to stop you in your tracks, "Woulda-Coulda-Shoulda." I would have started a business, but I should have applied for that job that I was qualified for, but you didn't. And now there's that nagging feeling of regret for not pursuing your dream, a regret of what might have been. Life is too short to be filled with regrets, what might have been, "Woulda-Coulda-Shoulda." Take your shot and leave it all on the field. I'd rather fail trying to reach my dream than to pass and leave it in the hands of someone who does not see what was planted in me, because I guarantee you that if you don't try, you will fail.

A VIEW FROM THE OWNER'S MANUAL

We have checked the view from Best Block USA, a view through a telescope, and a magnifying glass, from the road, and on top of a mountain, but let's check out the view from the owner's manual. When you want to know how something is supposed to operate, you should always refer to the owner's manual. It does not matter whether it's a car, television, or other electronic gadget or kitchen appliance, you should always read the manual. The manual will tell you the best way to care for and to operate that product. The manual will also tell you the best way to care for that product in order for it to operate a long time.

Well, there's a manual for us. In the beginning, God created the heaven and the earth. Everything that we have discovered, come to understand, have yet to understand, and have envisioned in our distant future was created in 6 days. And it started with the first recorded words of God, "Let There Be" and in the time span of thought, it was. God, the Great Architect of the Universe, saw the ending in the beginning and designed, developed, and built the necessary infrastructure, foundation, lighting, HVAC (heating and cooling), plumbing, and landscape. He set it on its 23^0 degree angle, started it rotating around the sun, and it is still doing what it was designed to do from the beginning.

Just as God has set the earth into motion, He designed,

made us, and breathed into us the breath of life, and man begin to live. He made us in His image and likeness. God gave us the ability to create, to imagine, and from that imagination, to design and build things that none of His other creations have been able to do. God has invested so much into man and thinks so much of us that He made us a little lower than the angels and has given us dominion over all the earth.

Just as this world of ours is on the move, so is man. We're moving from here to there and to and fro, coming and going. The world seems frantic about being there, wherever there is. Our values, self-worth, and vantage point in life are tied to what appears that we possess. Our definition of success is dictated by what car we drive, only because we cannot parade around in our homes. Our success is judged by the designer names that are plastered on the clothes we wear.

We are looking to the future, to where we want to be, but in order to get to that place in your future, you have to know where you are, and it's difficult at best to know where you are if you have no idea where you've been or from where you came. And, because we don't know, our vision has been skewed and our vantage point distorted.

The Holy Bible, our owner's manual, has been divinely given to man by God in order for man to realize not only who he is, but also whose he is in the blueprints of the Great Architect. This may sound overly simplistic and even cliché, but coming to and embracing your personal relationship with God will bring clarity to your perspective, outlook, and your vantage point when dealing with decisions you make daily.

Yes, the owners manual sets guidelines and boundaries for our operation, but these limitations optimize our potential, performance, and purpose.

I heard Doctor Miles Monroe speak in the Metropolitan Detroit area, where he made a comparison of putting gasoline or orange juice in the gas tank of your car. Dr. Monroe stated that no matter how much you may personally love orange juice and prefer to use it in your automobile, orange juice will not cause the necessary combustion in the engine to cause that engine to operate. As a matter of fact, it will cause damage and make that automobile inoperable, because the designers of your automobile designed it to operate with gasoline and placed what grade of gasoline is preferred for optimum performance in the owners manual.

The manufacturers have put their name on that automobile and will stand by their product because their reputation is on the line. The manufacturer will guarantee that automobile will operate properly, and if it fails to operate, you can bring it in and they will repair it.

God has placed a guarantee within the owners manual that if we follow the guidelines covered in the bible, we will perform optimally.

Joshua 1:7-8 (KJV)

> [7] *Only be thou strong and very courageous, that thou mayest observe to do according to all the law, which Moses my servant commanded thee: turn not from it to the right hand or to the left, that thou mayest prosper whithersoever thou goest.*

[8] This book of the law shall not depart out of thy mouth; but thou shalt meditate therein day and night, that thou mayest observe to do according to all that is written therein: for then thou shalt make thy way prosperous, and then thou shalt have good success.

If we do according to the owners manual and not turn from it, but embrace and meditate on it, we will prosper in whatever we do and find good success. This does not say fortune, fame or caviar dreams, but success. Not according to the standards set by the world, but by our manufacturer.

Now the world also offers alternative vantage points to obtain success and many of these options do not have the regulations attached that the owners manual has laid out. Taking this vantage point may provide you with some level of success. The success is not guaranteed and is short lived. But God, who is rich in mercy, stands by His guarantee eternally because His name is on us, and He has sent His Son to personally pay the cost to insure our success.

My journey has allowed me to view life through the lens of a child and an adult. I have viewed a close knit family, grown up on best block USA, and experienced the little church that did. I've seen a riot that cried no more, senseless assassinations of our leaders, a smoldering cross, and the Klan marching. I witnessed the election of the first black president, while bigotry is still raising its ugly head. I've seen a people rise up in the midst of tragedy and a nation rally together against terrorism.

God has seen fit to call me to shepherd a flock that has a

heart to do, when it was easier to fall in line with the status quo or to look the other way.

Along that journey was a thread consistently woven and connecting in the fabric of my hopes, dreams, and aspirations to erect a better vantage point, built on the foundation of Jesus Christ, the author and finisher of our faith and the co-author of the owners manual.

Through the good and the bad, the laughter and the tears, the triumphs as well as the disappointments, God is still there. He's been there since the beginning, and He's shedding that guiding light on the right path. He's giving comfort in those difficult moments. God said that I would never leave us nor forsake us. God continues to be there for those who choose to trust in Him. David's words ring true, *"I have been young and now I am old, but I've never seen the righteous forsaken, nor His seed begging bread".*

It is upon this platform that allows me to rise up and see a better way, where others see none. I am not blind to the challenges and obstacles that are present, but I hold onto the path walked by faith and not by sight.

www.ingramcontent.com/pod-product-compliance
Lightning Source LLC
LaVergne TN
LVHW051845080426
835512LV00018B/3083